GW01071823

Australian RICHARD SIMPKIN
LEGENDS

Australian
RICHARD SIMPKIN
LEGENDS

People whose story we should know

Foreword by Ray Martin

NEW
HOLLAND

First published in Australia in 2005 by New Holland Publishers (Australia) Pty Ltd
Sydney • Auckland • London • Cape Town

14 Aquatic Drive Frenchs Forest NSW 2086 Australia
218 Lake Road Northcote Auckland New Zealand
86 Edgware Road London W2 2EA United Kingdom
80 McKenzie Street Capte Town 8001 South Africa

Copyright © photographs and text: Richard Simpkin

All rights reserved. No part of this publication may be reproduced,
stored in a retrieval system or transmitted, in any form or by any means,
electronic, mechanical, photocopying, recording or otherwise, without
the prior written permission of the publishers and copyright holders.

National Library of Australia Cataloguing-in-Publication Data:

Simpkin, Richard P.
Australian legends : people who's story we should know.

Bibliography.
ISBN 1 74110 308 8.

1. Australia - Biography. I. Title.

920.094

Publishing Manager: Fiona Shultz
Project Editor: Lliane Clarke
Copy editor: Jenny Scepanovic
Designer: Norman Baptista, Nota Bene Design
Production Manager: Linda Bottari
Printer: Toppan, Hong Kong

10 9 8 7 6 5 4 3 2 1

To be great

in the future,

we must learn

about the greatness

of the past.

Richard Simpkin

Foreword

The eyes have it in these photographs. Forget what's wrapped around them. Forget the wrinkles and turkey necks, the bent backs and aches of old people. That's all part of weaving life's rich tapestry. Still, these 'character lines' almost disappear when you look into their eyes. The eyes have it.

That's where you see the Wisdom of the Elders. That's where you also catch the wit, the whimsy and the wonder of a Whitlam, Gough Esq. What a legend.

Mind you, they're all legends - every character in this picture pantheon is a legend.

Pick a number between one and eighty – between Alec Campbell (the Last Anzac) and Thomas Keneally (author) – and, you see the rich sparkle in their eyes.

Like Richard Simpkin, I've been privileged to meet most of these people. I was even witness to that moment when Richard flashed a few of these photographs. I saw Faith Bandler smile her beautiful smile, as she reflected and rejected racism at the launch of her autobiography. I heard Marcel Caux, as he waited for his first Anzac Day parade in a hundred year life, reject his war and every other war, as a terrible, tragic waste of life.

I also drank whisky with Alec Campbell and laughed at his Tasmanian compatriot, Frank McDonald, the last genuine hero from WWI. (He won the Military Medal, for his heroic madness one day on the Western Front, and he still didn't know why.)

Turn the pages 'til you find Jack Lockett, another old soldier, with the fine hands of a sculptor and the scars of a truly successful life. It's a splendid image.

Look at Sir Donald Bradman, with his bat and blue cardigan, posing on the front porch of his suburban Adelaide home. Such an ordinary setting for such an extraordinary man.

It's a camera style Richard has clearly adopted for this rich collection – mixing and matching the ordinary and extraordinary, in a most delightful way.

Sadly, some of these 'immortals' have moved on, since they paused for Richard's lens. Still, what he's done is preserve them, captured them if you like, so they can linger longer with us. Like all good clichés, or Chinese proverbs, there's a ring of truth to a picture being 'worth a thousand words.' A great picture moment is worth much, much than that.

Life, as we all know, is too fast these days. So it's rewarding to be able to press the Stop Button and catch a cheek-bone or a twinkle, of men and women who made a difference to who we all are and how we all live.

And these men and women all made a huge difference to Australia.

Imagine life without them. Imagine our sporting history without The Don, or Dawn, Herb or Heather. Imagine the arts without Dame Joan or Dame Edna, and the rest who graced the boards. From Bud Tingwell to Bart Cummings, from Joh Bjelke to Bruce Ruxton, love 'em or loath 'em, they've all enriched this landscape of ours. It would be a barren place without them.

This book pays tribute to them all. It's a colourful parade. An Australian kaleidoscope, if you like, of our recent past.

I must confess, along with forty years of journalism, I've also forked out a personal fortune to Mr Kodak, snapping a stock-house of pictures myself—of people and places, moments and memories—in a lifetime spent on the road.

My favourites in Richard's gallery are probably Nora Heysen, the prodigy with the palate from the Adelaide Hills, or John Laws, without the golden microphone. But, then, I really like his cluttered vision of Tom Keneally and I love Faith Bandler. Because I love Faith Bandler.

Ask me again in a month's time and I'd probably choose a different picture. But, that's what great pictures, like great paintings do. So, enjoy the journey.

And like I said, the eyes have it.

RAY MARTIN

Contents

Acknowledgements

FIRST, I must thank each and every one of the 80 Australian legends for cooperating with me for this book; they all took a gamble as I did not have a publisher when I met them all. Thank you to all of them for being part of my dream.

Samara, thank you for your love and support and for always believing that I would find the light at the end of the tunnel. And thank you for finding my lost words, for without words there would be no book. Grayem Linton, thank you for opening my eyes, especially about the war veterans, for without you I would only have 40 legends—it has been an amazing journey, but we made it! Thanks to New Holland Publishers, especially Fiona Schultz.

Kellie Edwards, thank you for getting me to Melbourne. Thanks to Glen-Marie Frost, Sarah Moffit, Jodie at 2UE, the Sanchez family for their continued support, Nola Simpkin for helping me financially (money makes the world go around), Noel Brown, Terry Coulits, Peter Carrette, the staff at RG Capital, Ray Martin, Kym Weatherley, Dr Paul Beaumont for keeping my eyes in focus, Christopher Lane, Rhett, Kell, Susie and Michael Hutchence for your support and friendship, my friends (you know who you are, I hope) and Uncle Paul.

The author with Sir Donald Bradman at his Adelaide home in 1995.

Introduction

I'VE BEEN asked why I have not included Australian legends such as Dame Nellie Melba and Banjo Paterson in this book. I agree that they are certainly legends, but sadly they passed away long before I was born. This is not a definitive list of Australian achievers; it is a collection of individuals whom I had the unique experience of actually meeting. I didn't want to write a book simply by doing research; I wanted to meet each individual for myself and try to understand how and why these people were so successful. I was fortunate enough to find out exactly why these eighty people have become Australian legends.

It sounds simple, but the reason most of these people are legends is because they had a dream and strove to achieve it—whether it was acting in Hollywood, writing best-selling books or flying aeroplanes. All of them either realised their dreams or did heroic acts and by doing so became Australian legends.

I originally had the idea for a photographic exhibition in 1996. I wrote a letter to Sir Donald Bradman, asking him if I could take a photo of him holding a cricket bat for an exhibition I had in mind called 'Australian Legends'. A month later I was on a plane to Adelaide and Sir Donald's home. My time with him was the most exciting forty-five minutes of my life. I thought to myself, if I can photograph Sir Donald Bradman, I can meet and photograph anybody. On my return, I wrote a list of names, off the top of my head, for my proposed exhibition. The list contained about ten people. I was only twenty-three at the time, so I didn't have much of an idea who to include.

Eventually I met and photographed all of the illustrious ten, but I obviously had to include more than ten people for such a significant exhibition. As time passed, I kept reading in the newspaper about Australian legends who had passed away. The papers would have a small picture and an article on the person and would very briefly skim through what they had achieved. I was amazed at some of the feats of these brilliant individuals and wondered why I hadn't heard of these remarkable Australians. The woeful thing is that after we close the newspaper and throw it away we forget about these unbelievable Australians and their triumphs.

I started to intensely research Australians and what they had achieved in all avenues of life. I was astounded to find out information about many Australians who had accomplished great things. For example, Dr David Warren, who in 1957 built the world's first cockpit-voice flight data recorder (commonly known today as 'the black box'), which is now in every plane throughout the world; Ray Lawler, who wrote the classic *Summer of the Seventeenth Doll*, which today is still playing throughout Australia, if not the world; and Nancy Bird Walton, who was Australia's first female aviator and also flew with Sir Charles Kingsford Smith.

I started sending out proposal letters to the individuals who I wanted to meet, photograph and interview for the exhibition. I was not commissioned by anybody to do this project, and had no backing from any organisations, so it was, to say the least, a struggle to meet these eighty individuals. But it was well worth it; as my friend Grayem Linton always tells me: 'You can buy an autograph, but how can you put a price on having afternoon tea with Sir Donald Bradman?' How true that is.

I interviewed more and more truly remarkable Australians and was astonished at how humble they were, and equally astounded by the fact that they were virtually unknown! We have so many outstanding Australians, yet we do not know about most of them until they pass away and we read about them in a daily paper, if we read about them at all.

I soon realised that I should have a book as well as an exhibition. A book that revealed who these people are and how they've lived their lives.

I have met, interviewed and photographed Australian legends who are instantly recognisable, as well as those who should be recognised. My aim is for my exhibition to travel throughout schools and country towns of Australia, so that children and adults start to take more of an interest in how great Australians can be. Regrettably, if you asked young adults who Errol Flynn or Dame Nellie Melba was, many would have no idea. I want to change this so that our current and future generations will know the names of the great Australians among us.

I truly hope that this book will be a part of Australian history, and that generation after generation can enjoy and be proud of the diverse and significant contributions that we as a people and nation have made.

I have travelled extensively throughout Australia to photograph these legends, but this book has also taken me to the United States to photograph Rod Taylor, an outstanding actor whom Alfred Hitchcock chose to star in the masterpiece *The Birds*. I have also crossed the globe to Italy and photographed Jeffrey Smart, who is respected worldwide for his remarkable modern art.

I hope that you appreciate the book's importance and learn about our great Australians. I hope that this book will be read by children in the future, and inspire them to achieve their dreams.

Creating this book has been a tumultuous journey at times, but also an incredible one, and I am very proud to have this opportunity to share it with you all.

Enjoy; I certainly did.

RICHARD SIMPKIN
December 2004

Eric Abraham

World War I veteran

ERIC KINGSLEY Abraham was born on 20 April 1898 in Queensland. In 1915 the Dungaree Recruiting March passed through Ipswich. This was the most famous recruiting march of World War I; the recruiters walked 160km from Warwick to Brisbane, gathering young men to fight in the war. 'I was seventeen and a half when I signed up for the army. They sent out fielders looking for recruitments. They asked me if I wanted to join, so I did. We signed up for the experience, to see what was happening, that's all. I had no interest in enlisting.'

Eric joined the 5th Division in Brisbane, where the Governor of Brisbane presented a bugle to his captain from the people of Brisbane, thanking the men for signing up. 'The captain asked us, can anyone play the bugle? There was no response, so I put my hand up. I learnt then and there to play the bugle!'

In March 1916 Eric and the rest of the 5th Division were about to leave for overseas. His friend asked if he could borrow his bugle. Eric agreed; and never saw it again—or so he thought!

Eric spent two months training in a Teleljibir camp before receiving orders to fight in France.

'Our captain told us to go to France and find and rejoin the 5th Division—don't ask questions just find it. We went to France and asked a fella where the 5th Division was; he had no idea, but told us to get on a train and get off at the last stop. Two days later we found them. I don't know how we found them, but we did.'

Eric and the rest of the men arrived in France during the coldest winter in memory. 'My first day in France was very cold. I had to carry a sandbag to where the fighting was taking place, and all of a sudden all hell broke loose— a huge explosion went off. I had never heard anything like it before—my knees buckled and I fell into a trench. A fella said, "You better not duck". I said, "I'm not ducking, I'm scared!"

'We continued on and delivered the items; when I got back to base a man said to me, "Don't worry, we all get scared." And that's the truth. If someone tells you that you don't get scared on the first day then they're lying.'

Eric saw much horror during his service in the Great War and he was involved in some of the cruellest battles in history, including operations at Villers Bretonneux, Morlancourt, the Battle of Amiens and the advance to Peronne, with the 5th Division Signals Company. Although Eric was involved in these famous battles, it was the Battle of Passchendaele that he considered the worst: 'Passchendaele was the worst action and shell fire I had ever seen. It was so bad that we were only allowed to fight four days at a time.'

Eric Abraham also witnessed the Red Baron going down. 'It was early morning and someone said, "The Red Baron is in the air!" He was manoeuvring around in his red plane, then out of the blue these machine guns went off and down went the plane. Everybody cheered. I never thought I'd see the day when I'd cheer when someone died.'

Discharged in October 1919, Eric felt that he was very lucky to come out of the war alive. 'Thank God I came home. All the war does is rob the community of good people. War is a strange thing; if I was somewhere a minute later or a minute earlier I could have been dead. That's how war was—it could have been you at any time.'

Eric passed away on 20 March 2003. I photographed him at his house in 2002. He had the funniest and most contagious laugh I had ever heard. As we were doing the photos Eric asked me if I would get his bugle out of his room. I said to him, 'It's a pity you lost your original bugle in 1916.' He then said to me, 'In April 2002, at my 104th birthday party, my friend gave me the original bugle that I gave away in 1916!' His friend had recently found it at some markets, so after 86 years, Eric and his bugle were reunited.

William 'Evan' Allen

World War I veteran

IN 1908 the American Navy visited Sydney. A young Evan Allen bought a few magazines about the navy and persuaded his father to take him to Sydney from his hometown of Bega to see the naval vessels. After that experience Evan wanted to join the navy. He was only nine at the time, but the experience of actually seeing a war ship changed his life forever.

Born William Evan Allen in 1899, Evan, as he likes to be called, joined the navy in March 1914, five months before World War I started. Like most men or boys who signed up to fight, he joined more for the adventure than to fight for king or country. Evan was only 14 and nine months old when he joined the navy and, like most boys of the time, he lied about his age. Evan, along with the rest of the 'boys', was taught seamanship, gunnery and how to use a rifle, with a bit of schooling thrown in.

When World War I broke out in August 1914, Evan was drafted to HMAS *Encounter*, a cruiser of 5600 tonnes. The *Encounter* was a lucky ship for Evan to be on, as during the entire war he never encountered the enemy. The *Encounter*'s main job was to patrol and protect the seas from the mainly German enemy, and to take Australian and New Zealand troops to Colombo. By the age of twenty-one Evan had accepted a promotion to chief petty officer, which was not looked upon as a positive thing to do by his fellow crew. Evan lost a lot of friends due to his promotion: in those days Australians did not like to take orders from others, and Evan had to exercise discipline.

When World War II broke out in 1939, Evan was still in the Australian Navy. Along with thousands of other men and women he again left the shores of Australia to fight the enemy on the other side of the world.

It was during World War II that Evan was reunited with a girl he had met in 1924, when he was in Vancouver, Canada. On 1 December 1941 Evan arrived once again in Vancouver, and was granted an extra day's leave to marry her.

Evan gave her his mother's address in Sydney and said, 'I don't know when I'll ever see you again. I'll have to say goodbye. The next day Evan sailed from Canada to San Francisco, where to his amazement his new wife was waiting.

Evan's life has been full of fortune. During World War II, he served time on the HMAS *Australia*, which was sent to the Admiralty Islands to fight the Japanese. However, Evan was assigned to another task, so he missed the HMAS *Australia* battle. When the ship returned, Evan greeted the captain and said: 'Sorry I missed you, sir.' 'You're a lucky man,' replied the captain. The HMAS *Australia* had come under heavy attack by five Kamikaze pilots. The man who was assigned to do Evan's job with the anti-aircraft guns was blown to bits.

Evan saw a lot more action during World War II and in 1947, after an amazing 34 years of service and two world wars, he finally retired from the Australian Navy.

After retiring, Evan and his wife bought a farm in Frankston, where they enjoyed the quieter life of farming. They were married for 40 years.

When I met Evan in his Melbourne nursing home in December 2000 he told me that he was the very last seaman still alive from World War I. He had an amazing memory—very precise—and was a lovely, humble and sweet man, who was proud that he could represent his mates who had passed away.

Faith Bandler

Activist

THE NAME Faith Bandler is a name that all Australians should know, but sadly do not! Faith is an Australian who has spent most of her life campaigning for Indigenous Australians to have the same legal rights as everyone else. Faith was initially driven to strive for equal opportunities for Indigenous Australians because her father, Wacvie Mussingkon, was kidnapped and sold to the British Empire as a slave. Mussingkon, along with about 60 000 slaves, helped establish the Australian sugar trade. In 1897 he escaped and settled in Tumbulgum, NSW. He married Ida and they had eight children, Faith being the seventh. 'Deep down, many Australians hate to think that their own country had slaves, but Aboriginal people were virtually enslaved, mostly on northern cattle stations.'

Faith Bandler was born in 1918. Her father died when she was only four years old. As a result, Faith was brought up by her mother, aunts and uncles. Faith left school at sixteen and made the move to Sydney. When World War II broke out, Faith served in the Australian Women's Land Army, working on farms growing food for the Australian troops. It was during this time that Faith realised that Aborigines weren't treated equally. Although she was doing the same work as her fellow workers, she and the other Aboriginal workers were getting paid less than the non-Aboriginal workers.

In 1951, Faith toured Eastern Europe and started getting actively involved in groups that were campaigning for Aboriginal rights. On her return, ASIO tapped her telephone and confiscated her passport for ten years. This was a turning point for Faith: 'It was a time when anyone who was talking about "rights" was automatically thought of as a communist,' she says.

In 1952, Faith married Hans Bandler. Hans showed compassion for Faith's cause; as an Austrian Jew, he had been imprisoned in a Nazi concentration camp during World War II.

Faith began campaigning for Aboriginal rights; she, along with Jesse Street and Perl Gibbs, founded the Aboriginal Australian Fellowship. The group's aim was to fight for Aborigines to be treated as equal to non-Aboriginal people. Before the referendum in May 1966, Australian Aborigines were not allowed to vote, were paid lower wages than non-Aboriginal people and were not allowed to travel freely in their own country, which they had lived in for thousands of years.

The year 1957 was an important year for Faith, Jesse and Perl. The year marked the commencement of the ten-year struggle for Aborigines to attain the same legal rights as non-Aboriginal Australians. Faith and others handed out petitions calling on the Australian Government to hold a referendum; thousands of black and white people signed the petition. In 1967 the government finally agreed to the long-overdue referendum. The referendum asked people to vote on whether they wanted the Australian Constitution changed so that Indigenous Australians had the same rights as other Australians. The Australian public voted yes by a huge 90 per cent.

'I saw people's passion rise during the 1967 campaign. There was a mighty force for something that was good.'

Faith is living proof that you can fight a government for equality and win. Since the 1967 referendum, Faith has continued to fight for the rights of Aborigines, Torres Strait Islanders and South Sea Island descendants, but she has not avoided controversy. In 1976, Faith was offered the MBE for services to the community, but declined due to the dismissal of former Australian Prime Minister Gough Whitlam. She did, however, accept the order of Australia in 1984 for services to Aboriginal welfare.

For several years I had been trying to photograph the elusive Faith Bandler; I had written to her on many occasions and spoken to her on just as many, with always the same response: 'No'. However, I was finally able to meet and photograph her at her book launch in 2002, and at the end of the day I went up to Faith and introduced myself. She smiled and added that she had thought I would be there. I got the feeling that Faith had wanted me to really fight for the opportunity to photograph her. She didn't want me to get my way, at least not without a fight.

Tom Bass

Sculptor

TOM BASS was born on 6 June 1916 in Lithgow, but the family moved around when he was a child because of his father's work. When Tom was eight his family were living in Gundagai. He had already taken a keen interest in art by this time and it happened that one day Dr Charles Gabriel went to visit Tom's next door neighbour. As he was entering the home a piece of paper flew up against the tree. The doctor, who was unknown to Tom and his friends, asked, 'Who drew this?'

'Tommy Bass,' replied the neighbour. Dr Gabriel was so impressed that he met with Tom's mother and told her that Tom was an artist. After several conversations, Tom was also convinced that he was an artist. However, it wasn't until he was 16 that he realised he wanted to become a sculptor. 'When I was sixteen I did a sculpture of a head; I had this material that looked like concrete, but it wasn't. It was exciting. I just had this impulse to carve it and I knew at that moment that I wanted to become a sculptor.'

In 1941, Tom was drafted into the army and spent most of his time working as a clerk in the district records office. During this time he married and had a child. When the war ended, he was delighted to find out that ex-servicemen were eligible for free training and education, so he enrolled at the National Art School in Sydney. He was excited about being able to sculpt full-time for three years. He graduated in 1948 and found the next few years tough, although he did acquire his first paid commission that year. He had to do odd jobs, such as collecting rubbish from golf courses and making models for department stores, to support his young family. He continued to create sculptures and in 1953 won a competition to do a sculpture for the University of New South Wales.

From there Tom's sculpting career really started, and he was soon being given commissions from all over Australia. Tom still feels that many of the works he completed in that period are very important. From the 1950s on, Tom was in demand; he was constantly working in Australia.

In 1962, Tom was commissioned to create a sculpture at the P&O building in Hunter Street, Sydney. In February 1963 it was featured on the front cover of OZ magazine.

Tom started teaching in the 1970s and it is something he still finds very important. 'In the early 1970s I felt like my career had come to an end. I was living in the country and had this urge to teach young people, so I could pass on my knowledge.' In 1974, he set up a private school, where he taught sculpture exclusively. Tom, now in his late 80s, is still teaching classes at his Sydney studio.

Despite his success as a sculptor he has been ignored by the art world, and that's exactly how he likes it. 'I never wanted to be represented in galleries. I don't see sculptures as belonging in galleries. I believe it is public art, social art. Sculptures should be outdoors where people can see them. Art galleries are for paintings, that's why they have walls; sculptures just don't fit in art galleries. People usually bump into them when they are walking back to look at a painting.'

Tom believes that there are two types of artists: 'There are the ones who become fascinated with the politics of art, who follow the art gallery circuit and try to fit in the art world. Then there are the other artists, who are just interested in their paintings and work. They are just what they are. It is not important for me to be recognised; the important thing is to be able to do what I want to. That's the important thing. Being recognised is not what it's all about.'

But Tom Bass is recognised, and he is regarded as one of Australia's most talented sculptors.

I met Tom in his Sydney studio in 2000. If Johnny Cash is the man in black, then Tom Bass is the man in white. He looks like a human sculpture. He is a reserved and unpretentious man who just wants to teach, sculpt and write poetry. I asked him to explain the word 'sculpture'. 'Sculpture is a language, just like English, French and German; it's something you translate into. You translate ordinary things into this language called sculpture.'

Graeme Bell

Musician

GRAEME EMERSON Bell was born on 7 September 1914 in Melbourne. As a child, Graeme and his brother, Roger, were surrounded by music; his mother Elva was a famous opera singer who toured with Dame Nellie Melba. His mother was regarded as the most promising young contralto voice to emerge from Australia. Melba told her to leave Australia and become a star overseas, but Elva's mother wouldn't allow it. Graeme's father, John, was in a musical comedy group. 'I grew up surrounded by music; it was a musical family,' says Graeme. When Graeme was eleven he was taught music by one of his mother's contemporaries, Jessie Stewart Young. 'Any expertise I have on the piano is due to Jessie.' When the Depression hit, Graeme was a teenager. It was very hard for his family to get by. 'We used to use old sheets as handkerchiefs and get our milk delivered in buckets.'

After completing school, Graeme gained a position at T & G Insurance as a clerk. He stayed there for nine years, hating every day. During this time his brother was bringing home American jazz records and introducing Graeme to the sounds of Fats Waller and Louis Armstrong. Before long, Graeme and Roger were scouring second-hand record shops, buying jazz records, taking them home and learning how to play them. Eventually they formed a small jazz band, but Graeme was more interested in art. He didn't intend becoming a jazz musician.

In 1943 Graeme was offered a job as band leader by Claude Carnell: his task would be to entertain the troops in Mackay. Graeme accepted and was happy that he could do something for the war effort. He was unable to go to war himself because of a chronic back condition. He stayed in Mackay for three months and worked at a club called the Coconut Grove in Brisbane, entertaining the American troops. However, he found that he could make more money selling alcohol to the troops than actually playing music. 'For some reason the Americans weren't allowed to buy grog, so we used to buy it for them and put it in our socks. They would pay us about five pounds for a bottle, while we were paying about 5 shillings!'

Graeme finally gave up his day job and worked as a musician, teaching music as a backup job. He formed his own music school and became quite successful as a teacher. In 1946 he accepted an offer to tour Czechoslovakia as part of the World Youth Festival; he sold his business and left for Czechoslovakia in 1947. This was to be the start of the Graeme Bell Dixieland Band. The tour was a huge success and the band was offered a recording contract. The press were writing feature stories about Graeme and his band in the papers, and on their return they were greeted at the docks by the media and fans. Graeme Bell was now a star. He started touring all around the world. 'I used to walk down the street with my son and people would say, "G'day Graeme" and I'd say, "Hi, how are you going" and my son would say, "Dad, who was that?" And I'd tell him that I didn't know! He was so confused at how all these people knew me and I didn't know them'!

Graeme continued to play sell-out shows around the world—he broke attendance records in London at the Hammersmith Palace. In 1951 he played for Princess Elizabeth at the Royal Festival Hall at the Royal Command Performance. Graeme then returned to Australia and had his very own jazz television show on Channel 7. It was during this time that he was able to interview Louis Armstrong, and the two become friends.

After 60 years and all of the changes in musical taste, Graeme Bell is still touring and recording.

I have photographed Graeme over several years (this photo was taken in 2000). In 2004 he played a sell-out tour for his ninetieth birthday. Graeme was remarkable, not just as a musician but as an entertainer. By the end of the show the crowd were dancing in the aisles. Graeme Bell had not lost his magic. One man yelled from the audience, 'Graeme, do you remember your old motto?' 'Remind me of it,' he replied. 'May we live long and die roaring,' the enthusiastic fan responded. Graeme still lives by that motto. I have been very privileged to witness that first hand, and cannot speak highly enough of him. He is a gentleman with great talent, and great enthusiasm for life.

Gilbert Bennion

GILBERT EDWARD Bennion was born on 1 October 1898. His father struck it rich in the gold rush and moved to Croydon. With the money Gilbert's father made from the gold mines he bought a machine that cut rock. The investment paid off and Gilbert's father struck a rich gold reef; he named it Lady Mary Reef of Croydon. Gilbert helped his father search for gold in the reef when he was a youngster. 'I had a wonderful childhood. It was full of happiness,' he remembers. In 1903 Gilbert attended Croydon State School, which he enjoyed very much.

In 1913, when Gilbert took a trip to visit his uncle and cousin in Townsville, his cousin picked him up in a car. It was the first time Gilbert had ever seen a car, and it was the only car in Townsville. 'I watched the horses react to this car; they didn't know what it was!'

Gilbert joined the cadets as a teenager and was soon promoted to sergeant, then second lieutenant. He served with the cadets in Townsville, while his brother was serving in France during World War I. 'I wanted to join the army and go to war but my parents didn't want me going over until my brother came home, just in case one of us died. They didn't want to lose both of their sons.' Some towns lost almost all of their young men—Gilbert's parents did not want to be a part of that statistic.

Gilbert started working at the railways, but he took leave in August 1918 and enlisted with the Australian Imperial Force in Townsville. Gilbert was elevated to corporal before joining the 5th Reinforcement. 'The government came to Enoggera and asked if someone had any experience in training. I had, so I volunteered to train about fifty men. I spent five months training the men at Enoggera. The army told us we were leaving soon for New Zealand, then Europe. I asked if I had time to say goodbye to my parents—I was granted a week. But when I returned, I was told that the boys had left for New Zealand the day before. I said, "Then I'll fly over tomorrow and meet them there." The next day the very first thing I saw in the papers was that the Japanese had surrendered to the Americans and I had missed the whole war. I still feel so ashamed that I missed that boat to New Zealand. I never saw any action.'

When the 51st Battalion was formed in North Queensland, Gilbert was promoted to lieutenant. He carried out his duties with the Mareeba Militia for seven years. After his time with the army Gilbert went back to the railways and became station master for thirty-five stations. 'It was a lifetime duty,' he says. He worked for the railways for fifty-one years and was the last station master at Tweed Heads.

'After I retired from the railways, the post office wanted me to work for them as post master. I had to say no, but I knew it was a compliment to me.' Gilbert loved his job working for the railways and became multi-skilled by learning how to type, do Morse code and take shorthand.

Before he died in 2005, Gilbert was one of only four surviving diggers from the 330 000 Australians who enlisted in the 'war to end all wars'. More than half of our troops who 'went for the adventure' were killed or wounded, which was disastrous for such a young and vulnerable country. It was, in fact, the largest loss for any fighting nation. And as a nation we must appreciate and honour their spirit, just as Gilbert Bennion did.

When Gilbert passed away in January 2005 he was 106.

When I met Gilbert in August 2004, he was just about to turn 106 and was in good spirits. Unfortunately he still felt extremely guilty that he had missed out on serving his country in World War I. Gilbert may never have seen action during World War I, but that doesn't matter. He served his time training to serve our country and dedicated his life to the railways. For me, Gilbert had a wonderful hearty laugh that I'll treasure forever.

Sir Joh Bjelke-Petersen

Former Queensland premier

SIR JOH was born Johannes Bjelke-Petersen in New Zealand on 13 January 1911. When Johannes was two his family moved to Kingaroy, an area north-west of Brisbane. Joh worked in Kingaroy as a peanut farmer, and it was during his time as a farmer that he became interested in politics.

In 1946 Joh was elected as a Country Party member of the Queensland Legislative Assembly.

He worked his way up in the Country Party, and in 1957 the Liberal Party and Country Party coalition came into power in Queensland. Joh was a minister from 1963 until 1968 and was then elected leader of the Country Party, and therefore Premier of Queensland on 8 August 1968. One of the first things that Joh and his government achieved was the abolition of state death duties. This opened the flood gates to Queensland, especially Surfers Paradise, for retirees, mainly from the southern states of Australia.

For good (economic) or bad (density of population), Surfers Paradise boomed during the 1970s and 1980s. With great weather and no state death duties, many Australians chose Surfers Paradise as either their retirement or holiday destination. The developments around Surfers Paradise are due to Joh's vision to expand Queensland; that expansion has now lasted for thirty years.

During his time as premier, Joh's government became well known for having a strong hold over the state of Queensland. From early on he disliked protestors, banning them from any rallies unless they were authorised. He was not afraid to use the police to break them up either. Bjelke-Petersen was a strong politician who was never scared of a fight. Whether it was his political opponents, protestors or the press, Joh loved to stay in control. When he was confronted with questions from the media, Joh would often dismiss them with his famous quote: 'Don't you worry about that.' Ultimately, it was Joh who would have to worry.

In 1974 Bjelke-Petersen changed the name of the Country Party to the National Party. There were whispers that Joh's government was corrupt, and the television program *Four Corners* aired a story about the possible corruption in Joh's police force. This led to a two-year investigation of Joh's government, headed by barrister Tony Fitzgerald (the Fitzgerald Inquiry), which tore open the government. The police commissioner and numerous government ministers were convicted of corruption and sentenced to prison. Bjelke-Petersen was stood down as National Party leader on 26 November 1987, but refused to resign as premier. Instead, Bjelke-Petersen asked Governor Sir Walter Campbell to dismiss all the other ministers in his government. Campbell refused Joh's request and he resigned as Premier of Queensland on 1 December 1987.

After almost 20 years as the state's premier, Joh could not retire in Queensland in peace, like most Australians. The Fitzgerald Inquiry had led to a criminal prosecution against Joh for perjury. Many experts now say that Joh was in fact naive about what was happening in his government and that he was not corrupt at all. Corrupt or not, Bjelke-Petersen became known to most Australians for being corrupt, rather than for his achievements in Queensland. Eventually prosecutors decided not to attempt any further action against Joh, due to his deteriorating health and his age. Dismissed without his pension, Joh and his family have opened up their house to visitors on an almost daily basis and make a small living from the tourist groups.

I travelled to Sir Joh's farm in Kingaroy in 2002. After navigating a few cows, I was led onto the property by Sir Joh's son and warmly greeted by Lady Flo Bjelke-Peterson. A short time later Sir Joh came out on his electronic wheelchair. He was not in good health, but could still tell a joke. After photographing him in the scorching Queensland sun, I asked him if he was all right. In a soft and weak voice, he answered with a smile, 'Don't you worry about that!'

Charles Blackman

Artist

CHARLES BLACKMAN was born in Sydney in 1928. He studied at the East Sydney Technical College from 1943 to 1946. His first paid job was for the *Sun* newspaper, where he worked for five years. In 1952 he moved from Sydney to Melbourne to become a full-time artist. It was during this time that he began to notice schoolgirls' hats. In 1954 Charles held an exhibition in Melbourne that featured the series of schoolgirls and their hats; it caused a lot of debate, but it was his subjects that made him famous. 'Where I lived in Hawthorn, there were a lot of schoolgirls, and at 3 o'clock when the schoolgirls used to get on the trams I noticed there were a lot of hats, and hats seem to represent something. So I started painting a series of hats to see if anybody liked them, but it caused a lot of controversy. No-one could understand why I wanted to paint schoolgirls. They thought I was a weirdo, but I'm not a weirdo.'

Weirdo or not, Charles had made a name for himself in the art world; not just in Australia but around the world. Charles left Australia for London, where he and fellow artist Arthur Boyd lived near each other; they spent a lot of time painting together and Boyd taught Charles to 'economise'. Boyd and Charles used to buy second-hand canvases, clean them, stretch them and re-use them. Charles returned to Australia, where he had many exhibitions and won numerous prestigious awards for his paintings. He became famous not only for his 'schoolgirl' paintings, but also his *Alice in Wonderland* series. Charles describes the *Alice* paintings as 'like an eccentric child escaping into my own mind'. In 1959 Charles was awarded the Rowney Prize for drawing. He followed that with a successful exhibition at the Johnson Gallery. In 1962-63 he was part of London's Tate Gallery exhibition of Australian artists.

In 1977, Charles received an OBE for services to art and in 1993 the National Gallery of Victoria in Melbourne put together the first retrospective of Charles's work, 'Schoolgirls and Angels'. The exhibition went to Sydney, Brisbane and Perth. Charles is very honest with his thoughts, noting that certain art galleries have his work, 'but you have to go into the dungeon to see it. If the director of the gallery doesn't like your work then he won't show it.'

When I asked Charles what he thought about art today he gave me an honest answer: 'If you go to university and you draw a line down the middle of a page, the space either side of the line has to be explained in a thesis. If you're going to explain why the line is down the middle and you can explain the vacant spaces either side, then you graduate—but it ain't art! Painting takes a long time to do. It's like life itself: you spend a lot of time thinking about what you are doing with your feelings. If your feelings are right then you'll be spot on.'

Charles must have had good feelings about his art. For most of his life he has been one of Australia's most talented and famous artists. Now in his seventies and not in the best of health, his carer and friend Fred looks after 'Charlie' for almost nothing. For Fred it's an honour to take care of Charles; for most of us, it's simply an honour to see one of his paintings.

Charles has had ups and downs in his personal life but still has a great personality and has remained very down to earth. He may not have the luxuries that his fellow artists live with, but that's okay with him: 'Money has never meant a lot to me; aspiration, how you paint, and what you paint means the most to me.'

Blackman is a real artist. He doesn't create art for money, he creates art for art's sake.

On one of the occasions that I photographed Charles at his house, I commented that I liked one of his sketches. Charles then got a piece of paper and pen and drew me an angel. 'There you go mate,' he said. I was very excited and said to him 'You don't have to do that.' 'I know,' replied Charles, 'but I know you'll appreciate it.'

Sir Donald Bradman

Cricketer

THE NAME Don Bradman conjures up a sense of pride in any Australian. What exactly did he do that was so special? Why is he so loved by not only the people who saw him play, but also the young kids of today? We all know of his remarkable average of 99.94 runs in Test cricket—almost double the average of his nearest counterpart. When asked why he was better than everybody else, Bradman simply answered, 'I don't know.' There have been many books written trying to analyse all aspects of his game. In fact, he himself wrote the classic *How to Play Cricket*. After all the analysing that has been done, commentators still can't reach a conclusion—they probably never will. To most cricket lovers in Australia and around the world, he was a god. To the average person on the street he was an icon. You don't have to know anything about cricket to have heard of Don Bradman.

Donald George Bradman was born at Cootamundra, NSW on 27 August 1908. He made his first-class debut for NSW against South Australia on 16 December 1927. He made his Test debut against England on 30 November 1928. On 6 January 1930 Bradman scored a massive 452 not out for NSW against Queensland in only 377 minutes, with an impressive 49 fours. His highest score in a Test was against England on 12 July 1930, where he scored 334 in only 383 minutes. Surprisingly, Bradman could also bowl. On 15 December 1930 he took his first Test wicket (Ivan Burrow, lbw). His first-class bowling figures are 36 wickets for 1367 runs, with an average of 37.97. An impressive statistic for the man known as the greatest batsman of all time.

In 1932, Bradman married his childhood sweetheart Jessie Menzies. Bradman described their 65-year marriage as 'the greatest partnership of my life'. In 1934, Bradman moved from NSW to South Australia and played Sheffield Shield for that state, until his retirement from cricket in 1948-49. From 1939 to 1946 Bradman did not play Test cricket due to World War II. In 1948, at the age of 40, Bradman led his team to England, winning every match, including all five Test matches. The Invincibles, as they were known, are regarded as the greatest Australian Test team of all time. In August 1948, Bradman played his last Test innings. He was bowled for 0. Unknown to Don, he had needed just four more runs to have an average of 100. On 5 March 1949 Bradman played his last innings in first-class cricket and scored 30 runs. In his career, he would score 1 four hundred, 5 triple hundreds, 31 double hundreds and 117 hundreds. He is the only Australian with 100 hundreds. He averaged a century every 2.8 innings.

At the peak of his fame he was receiving thousands of fan letters each week. While the rest of his teammates spent time at the hotel bar, Bradman was in his room answering his letters. He would have a few hours' sleep, then go out the next morning and score the odd hundred or two! Historians note that when Bradman was playing in the early 1930s during the Great Depression, his batting lifted the spirits of the entire nation. Bradman's own teammates were in awe of him. A typical example is Ian Johnson, a former captain of Australia and a member of the 1948 Invincibles. Johnson had a typed letter from The Don which was over 50 years old—framed and proudly displayed in his lounge room.

When Sir Donald Bradman passed away on 25 February 2001, cricketing nations around the world mourned as one. Grown men were ringing up radio stations crying. A proud and teary-eyed John Howard told us all that as a child he had watched Sir Donald play. It has been statistically proven that Bradman was the greatest athlete of all time—even better than American baseball greats Babe Ruth and Joe DiMaggio. Bradman may be gone, but he will never be out.

In 1995 and 1996, I was fortunate enough to meet Sir Donald Bradman. On one occasion I arrived at his home just after a group of schoolchildren had been sitting on the front steps, with Sir Donald helping them answer questions about himself for their school project. He was more than just the greatest cricketer of all time; he was a remarkable human being.

Arthur 'Scobie' Breasley

Jockey

ARTHUR 'SCOBIE' Breasley was born in Wagga Wagga, NSW in 1914. As a child Arthur was very interested in horses; he knew from a young age that he wanted to become a jockey. This resulted in a family friend nicknaming him after the famous horse trainer James Scobie. When Arthur was just 12 his older brother, who was a jockey in Melbourne, sent for him. Scobie left school and moved to Melbourne, where he became an apprentice to trainer Pat Quinlan at Caulfield.

In 1928, when he was 14, Scobie rode and won his first professional race in Melbourne—and had a very bad fall. 'I got badly injured in 1928. I got a fractured skull, lost my balance and went cross-eyed for a while. They didn't tell me this, but the doctors told my trainer that I would never ride again. I was back on a horse in three months.'

In 1929, at the age of 15, Scobie rode in his first Melbourne Cup against the greatest horse of them all —Phar Lap. 'He was a great horse, one of the best I've ever seen.'

Scobie rode in a number of Melbourne Cups but never won it. Incredibly, Scobie finished in the top five, eight times. The Melbourne Cup always eluded him, but he did come very close: 'I rode Shadow King in 1933, but got badly interfered with coming into the straight and came a close second. Otherwise I would've won it; I came second again on a horse called Target, and another year I was offered to ride a horse called Serious. I would've taken it, but I had taken a horse the day before. Serious ended up winning the Melbourne Cup, so I should have won a few Melbourne Cups. But it doesn't matter—I won every other major race.'

Scobie started winning race after race, and in 1942 he won the Caulfield Cup on Tranquil Star. He won the race again in 1943, 1944, 1945, and 1952. To this day Scobie still holds the record for the most wins in the Caulfield Cup. Scobie was also the Victorian Premier Jockey in three consecutive years, from 1944 to 1946.

When Scobie turned 35 he felt that he needed a change. He and his wife May wanted to travel overseas and have a look at the world. 'I told my friend that I would like to ride overseas, and he came back with two offers. So we left for England.' Scobie had huge success riding in England; he was England's champion jockey four times (1957, 1961, 1962, and 1963). Scobie won the King George VI and Queen Elizabeth Stakes, the Prix de L'Arc de Triomphe in France and the Eclipse Stakes, all on Ballymoss. However, his biggest win was the 1964 English Derby—by which time he was a 50-year-old grandfather.

'The greatest thrill I ever got out of winning was my first English Derby, in 1964, on a horse called Santa Claus. I said he was my Santa Claus—I was very proud of that win.' Breasley won the English Derby again in 1966 on Charlotte Town. In 1966 Scobie won five races out of six starts at Lewes, England.

Scobie's career spanned over 40 years. He retired in 1968 at the age of 54. He rode 3251 winners—1091 in Australia and 2160 overseas, predominantly in England. After retiring from racing, Scobie became a horse trainer in England, France, America, India and Barbados. Today Scobie still holds the record of four Cockspun Gold Cups in Barbados. Scobie eventually returned home to Australia and in 1996 Racing Victoria introduced the Scobie Breasley Medal, which is awarded to the best Victorian jockey of the year. 'Naming that medal after me made me feel wonderful. I'm very proud and honoured.'

I met Scobie Breasley in 2000 at his Melbourne home. He had numerous photos and paintings of his racing days and even a letter from the Queen Mother. 'I won for the Queen, as well as the Queen Mother,' he told me proudly. I also noticed his black slippers, fit for a king, with the initials 'SB' embroidered in gold; they seemed out of place in his humble home. However, in the sport of kings, Scobie Breasley is definitely a king.

Alec Campbell

Last survivor of Gallipoli

O F ALL the soldiers who enlisted in World War I, Alec Campbell became the face of Gallipoli. He didn't want to serve, nor did he really understand why he was fighting, but history books will show that Alec William Campbell would be the last man standing of those who served in Gallipoli.

Alec Campbell was born on 26 February 1899. On 2 July 1915 Alec reported to the recruiting office to sign up for the Great War. Alec enjoyed riding horses and wanted to be in the Light Horse Brigade, but was told there was a waiting list. He was afraid that he might miss the war, so he joined the Australian Imperial Force instead. Alec was 16 and four months, but told the recruiting officers that he was 18 and four months. After convincing the recruiting officers of his age, he had to persuade his parents to sign a letter giving consent for him to go off to war. On 30 June 1915, Alec's parents signed the document.

Private A.W. Campbell, no. 273, 15th Battalion, Fourth Infantry Brigade AIF, as he was now known, sailed on 15 August 1915 aboard the SS *Kyarra*. After arriving in Egypt, he and his mates trained in the sand dunes of Cairo: 'It was all an adventure; it was amazing to see the pyramids, camels and sand dunes.'

After training in Egypt, Alec left for the shores of Gallipoli. During his journey there, a man sitting in front of Alec was shot by a Turkish sniper and fell to the floor of the boat. Alec arrived, shaken, in Gallipoli in October 1915. 'When we arrived there was rapid fire. You had to keep your head down or you would get shot. I remember it being very hilly; we had to build trenches where we would fire from. Most of the firing would be done from the trenches, and we would just blaze away.'

Alec first joined the army, like many, for the adventure. 'When I was there it was sort of an adventure in a way, because I was young, you see. I was too young to think of war as a wrong thing. Overall it was a dangerous place to be and we were glad to come home.' Alec saw just six weeks' service in Gallipoli.

On 3 January 1916 Private Campbell was admitted to the First Australian General Hospital in Cairo. His health had completely broken down and he spent six months in Cairo recovering. He had jaundice, scabies, head lice, mumps and palsy, which permanently paralysed the right-hand side of his face. On 24 June 1916 Alec boarded the *Port Sydney* and headed home. On his arrival in Tasmania he was discharged from the army as being medically unfit.

Alec's life after Gallipoli was long and full. He went bush and was a jackaroo, and he spent time building houses, which gave him his strength and overall health back. He became the Tasmanian Flyweight Boxing Champion, spent time building boats, and worked on building the first Parliament House in Canberra (which opened in 1927). Alec got married, had children and worked for the railways. In his fifties, Alec gained a university degree in economics. He also learnt to sail and competed in six Sydney to Hobart races.

Alec remarried and had two more children—his last when he was 69—and later worked as an advisor for the National Heart Foundation until he was in his 80s. Despite having lived a life definitely filled to the brim, Alec William Campbell will be most remembered for his services in Gallipoli.

The entire nation mourned as one on Thursday, 16 May 2002, when Alec passed away.

I was lucky to spend two days with Alec and his wife Kathleen in February 2002. I spent time interviewing and photographing him. His memory of his days spent at Gallipoli had almost gone, and it was just as well; Gallipoli was no place for anyone to fight in 1915, especially a 16-year-old boy. I asked Alec 'Do you feel proud to have been part of Gallipoli?' 'No,' he said, 'it never struck me to be proud. Why should I be?' Alec embodied the true Anzac spirit; he was, and always will be, our digger.

Judy Cassab

Artist

JUDY CASSAB was born on 15 August 1920 in Vienna, Austria. In 1929 Judy's parents divorced and Judy returned to Hungary, where she was brought up by her grandparents. At a young age Judy showed a tremendous ability to draw people; she painted her first portrait of her grandmother when she was just twelve. After completing school Judy married Jancsi Kampfner in 1939, but life was about to take a turn for the worse: World War II had begun and spread across Europe. Judy's husband was captured by the Nazis and taken to a labour camp in Poland, and her mother was taken to Auschwitz. Judy moved to the safety of Budapest, where she studied art.

While attending art school, Judy's art teacher told her to stop painting. 'I painted this beautiful portrait of a lady that I was very proud of. I showed it to my art teacher. She told me it was terrible and that I should stay away from portraits. It was on that day that I became an artist.' In 1944, with the war still raging across Europe, Judy took on a new identity to avoid being captured by the Nazis. When the war ended, Judy was lucky to be reunited with her husband.

In 1947 Judy had an exhibition at the National Salon in Budapest. Although she was painting, the war had taken a heavy toll on her and her husband. They had just started a family and they needed a change. It was fate that Judy and her family ended in Australia. 'We made up our minds in Vienna; people would sit in coffee houses and spin the globe around. We didn't want to go anywhere with the same social issues as Hungary. We applied to Canada and Australia. We waited two years for a reply; Australia replied first.

Judy and Jancsi arrived in Australia in 1951. Judy wanted to get a job working in a factory, but her husband knew that what she really wanted was to become an artist; he didn't want her to work in a factory. 'He didn't want a frustrated wife.' So Judy started painting again, but because she was not bringing in any money into the house she felt like a burden.

In 1953, Judy had her first exhibition at the Macquarie Gallery in Sydney. She sold several paintings at eight pounds each. The average wage at the time was seven pounds a week, but it wasn't a regular income. Judy was making a name for herself, but not enough to earn a living. She started teaching art as well as selling her paintings. Judy could now afford a housekeeper. As she didn't have to wash, iron, cook and clean the house, she was able to concentrate on her art full-time. Judy was now making a name for herself in the art world. She became friends with other well-known and respected artists and started painting their portraits. In 1957 she became an Australian citizen.

In 1960 Judy entered her portrait of fellow artist and friend Stanislaus Rapotec into the Archibald Prize. The judges delayed the winning announcement by a few hours because they couldn't decide on a winner. Judy received a phone call from the curator of the NSW Art Gallery, Daniel Thomas: 'Judy, you have just won the Archibald.' She was only the second woman to win the illustrious award. Seven years later Judy won her second Archibald Prize with a painting of friend and fellow artist Margo Lewers. She was by then very much part of Australian history.

Judy Cassab is regarded as Australia's best female portrait painter and is still the only woman to have won the Archibald twice.

I met and photographed Judy in 2004, and she gave me a tour of her apartment, which was full of art. She said of her portraits: 'I like to paint one eye smiling, one eye sad; it transcends reality.' One painting caught my eye. 'Can you tell me about that one?' I asked. Judy happily agreed. 'When I was at school I drew all of my school friends' faces with the headmaster, who we all adored. When the war broke out in Austria the school was burnt down to the ground.' Judy thought the drawing had been destroyed, but about 15 years ago she received it in the mail. The headmaster's daughter had rescued the drawing from the burning school, and after 40 years, Cassab was reunited with her drawing.

Marcel Caux
World War I veteran

At the end of Marcel Caux's long life, he was one of the most famous people in Australia: he was one of only five World War I veterans who were still alive in Australia. He appeared on numerous newspaper front pages and became a talking point for many Australians. However, for most of Marcel's life, he wanted to remain anonymous.

Born Marcel Caux in Gladesville on 1 March 1899, he enlisted in the army at the age of 16. Like a lot of his peers, he deliberately raised his age because, as he puts it, 'I didn't have anything else to do.' Marcel sailed with the 17th Battalion and then trained in the hot and sandy surrounds of Egypt. Marcel joined the 20th Battalion and was sent to the Somme in France, where he served in possibly the most horrific trenches of the Western Front.

In 1916 Marcel was wounded in the Battle of Pozires. He recovered only to be wounded in the Battle of Hangard Wood, and in 1918, while fighting in the Battle of Villers Bretonneux, Marcel was shot in the knee. Because of this injury, Marcel was sent back home to Australia; he was unable to bend that leg for the rest of his life.

Once back home in 1919, Marcel was not treated with the respect he deserved by the Australian Government. Due to the injuries that he had sustained while fighting, he needed medical treatment. He asked for help with his medical bills and unemployment benefits, but the government denied his requests, telling him that if he could stand up, there was nothing wrong with him. Marcel had had enough. He ripped up all of his service photos, and threw away his medals and all documents that reminded him of World War I. He had fought for a country that was not willing to fight for him.

Marcel was mentally and physically scarred for life. He wanted to forget everything about the war, so he 'went bush'. He learnt to be a carpenter and shipbuilder—he didn't retire until he was 85. He created a whole new identity for himself, and told people that he was ten years younger than he really was.

During the 1950s Marcel got married and had a son, Marcus. When his son and wife asked Marcel about his injured leg, Marcel told them that it happened in World War II; he thought it was more acceptable than to tell people he had been in World War I. Marcel's wife, Doris, and his son believed he was ten years younger than he actually was.

In 1998 the French Government presented him with the Legion d'Honeure on the eightieth anniversary of Armistice. Marcel didn't confirm his involvement in World War I until his wife had died. His son Marcus was as shocked as anyone else.

In 2001, aged 102, Marcel attended a Remembrance Day ceremony. When asked what he thought about the Great War he answered: 'I'd rather forget the whole bloody thing.' In 2002, aged 103, Marcel attended his first Anzac Day march. That was where I noticed him and photographed him. Within moments of me photographing him, Marcel was noticed by the media, who then photographed and interviewed him. The next day he appeared in all of the papers.

The next Anzac Day march, in 2003, Marcel was surrounded like a movie star, with everyone crowding around his car. The following year in 2004 Marcel once again attended the Anzac Day march and once again the media and public surrounded him, asking him about the Great War and what he thought about Australia's involvement in Iraq. Adults and children gathered around him, just to say thank you and to shake his hand. It was to be Marcel's last Anzac Day march. With a smile and a wave to the crowd, Marcel said goodbye to the people of Australia. He passed away on 22 August 2004, aged 105. Marcel Caux was finally allowed to Rest In Peace. We will remember him.

In May 2002 I went to visit Marcel in his Chatswood nursing home; I photographed him and interviewed him about World War I. 'Why do you want to know about that?' he asked me. I told him that it was part of history and so was he. Marcel replied, 'I'd rather forget about it [World War I]; it's ruined my whole life.' But he added that he wanted to stick around for next year's Anzac Day march, as it was important for the children to learn that war was no good.

Eddie Charlton

Snooker player

EDDIE CHARLTON was born on 31 October 1929 in Merewether, NSW. Eddie was an amazing all-round athlete; his only trouble was deciding which sport he wanted to dominate. He was a first grade cricketer and tennis player, represented Newcastle in soccer and rugby, was an amateur boxer, surfer, swimmer and, of course, a snooker player. However, before Eddie became a household name for his snooker achievements, he spent 22 years in the coal mines of Awaba, NSW, working underground for 15 of those hard years. At the very young age of fourteen, Eddy was working as a miner, playing snooker and beating most of the men in the town.

In 1948, when Eddie was only eighteen, he played an exhibition match with Australia's (if not the world's) greatest billiards player of the time, Walter Lindrum. Eddie won the game, but has always believed that Lindrum let him win. Eddie had shown first-class skills in an amazing nine sports, and was asked to carry the Olympic torch through Swansea, on its way to Melbourne for the 1956 Olympic Games.

The year 1960 would become an important year in Eddie's professional life. When Fred Davis, the world professional snooker champion, toured Australia, he noticed the potential in Eddie and convinced him to take up snooker as a professional. Eddie broke into the world snooker circuit and in 1968 won the World Open Snooker Championships; he won this event for ten years consecutively. It was a good time to be on top of the game because in 1969 snooker began to be televised on the BBC *Pot Black* program. Eddie was regularly seen on British and Australian television.

In 1972, 1973 and 1980 Eddie was the *Pot Black* champion; he went on to win almost every major snooker championship that existed. However, the World Professional Snooker Championship escaped his trophy cabinet. He was runner-up in 1968, 1973 and 1975. He was also runner-up at the World Professional Billiards Championship in 1974, 1976 and 1984.

Eddie had the nickname of Steady Eddie because of his concise and conventional game. For twelve consecutive years, Eddie's world ranking was in the top three. The year 1976 was good for Eddie; he shot an unbelievable snooker score with a break of 147 points, and also won the World Matchplay Championships against his arch rival Ray Reardon; he considers this his greatest achievement. In an amazing 20-year dominance, from 1964 to 1984, Eddie won the Australian Professional Championship every year, except for 1968.

Eddie was not just a great snooker and billiards champion; he also brought major players to our shores for Australian tournaments and was vital in implementing Australia's first professional championships for 30 years. At the age of 55, he was still ranked sixth in the world, and in his mid-seventies Eddie played in the World Seniors Masters—he was the world's senior runner-up in 1991.

Eddie was a great champion and a great person. People still ask me, what it was like to have dinner with the great Eddie Charlton and my answer is: 'It's like playing snooker with him. The balls have a place, which is in the pockets, and dinner was the same. Everything was in the right place.'

Eddie Charlton died in November 2004 aged 75.

I met Eddie in 2001 at his local RSL. 'Six o'clock' he said. I arrived at 5:45pm and wanted to know if he was already there, so I asked a lady who was working there. 'What time is it?' she asked. '5:45pm', I replied. 'Don't worry, he'll be here at 6pm on the dot; he always is,' she said. True to his word, at the stroke of 6pm Eddie arrived with a cue and a friendly handshake. We went downstairs to the billiards room and he hit the balls around while I took some photos. After the photo shoot he kindly invited my friend and me to dinner—we had a great night.

Ron Clarke

Athlete

RONALD WILLIAM Clarke was born in Melbourne on 21 February 1937. As a teenager Ron showed tremendous athletic ability—not only on the track but also as a VFL player. He played Aussie Rules as a junior, inspired by his father, who played for Essendon. As a child, Ron and his older brother (who ended up playing first grade for Essendon) used to hang around the Essendon footy players, but during a game of Aussie Rules one day Ron broke his finger and decided to take up running again. When he was 16 he broke the school's under-17 mile and 880 yards records, and within three years had set the world junior mile record; 4 minutes 6 seconds. In 1956 Ron was secretly chosen to be the final torchbearer at the Melbourne Olympics—a bittersweet moment. 'When I got to the top and lit the cauldron I remember thinking to myself that it would be a good view to watch the footy from. I would rather have been down there competing as an athlete. Marjorie Jackson should have been the torchbearer, not me.' Ron thinks of that time as a famous photo more than anything else: 'It did nothing for my running career.'

Ron practically retired for four years when he worked full-time, got married and bought a house. He was then chosen for the 1964 Tokyo Olympic Games, and ran in the 10 000 metres, winning a bronze medal. But it was in the following year that Ron stamped his name on world athletics. In Oslo, Ron was the first athlete to run under 28 minutes for 10 000 metres; his world record is still looked upon as one of the greatest athletic feats of all time. While touring the United States and Europe, Ron won thirteen out of seventeen races and set six world records, but the highlight of Ron's career was the English Three Mile: 'It was July 1965 and the English mile was a race that had all of the best mile runners from around the world. I won the race and broke the 13 minute barrier for three miles.'

In 1965, Ron was voted ABC Sportsman of the Year and BBC World Sportsman of the Year. In 1966 he was French Academic Sportsworld Sportsman of the Year. Ron had won everything except an Olympic gold. In 1968 he was once again picked for the Australian athletics team.

The Olympics were held in Mexico City, which is 2340 metres above sea level. Ron was still working full-time as an accountant and was only allowed one month for preparation. He flew out to Mexico and began to adjust his body to the altitude. In reality, he needed more than a month, but he had a family and a job, and he was an amateur athlete not a professional.

The high altitude played a major role in the race—runners were dropping like flies and being carried from the track on stretchers. Three laps to go and Ron was with the front pack; with 600 metres to go Ron made a move, hoping to create a gap between him and the other runners, but into the last 400 metres Ron started to slow down and the other runners slowly passed him—Ron was running on empty. As Ron came down the straight, the team doctor, Dr Brian Corrigan, knew something was wrong. He jumped over the fence with oxygen. When Ron crossed the line in sixth place he collapsed. He lay on the track under a blanket, being given oxygen for ten minutes, his arms and legs jerking. The doctor cried, as he knew Ron was in trouble. The athletes and crowd were stunned; the race favourite was unconscious. After ten minutes Ron came to, got up and with assistance walked off the track. Later he found out that he had a defect in his heart, which had probably prevented him from obtaining that elusive gold. In 1982, the defect in his heart had become so serious that he had to undergo heart surgery to save his life.

Though he broke 18 world records, Ron never won an Olympic gold—it's almost like Bradman not getting an average of 100, but that's history. Gold medal or not, Ron Clarke remains one of the greatest athletes of all time.

I met Ron Clarke in his offices in Melbourne in 2002. He was very welcoming and cleared his afternoon, which was full of meetings, to spend some time with me. He was extremely modest and had a good sense of humour. 'How many times have you been asked about not winning a gold medal?' I asked. 'Oh, about two million!' he replied with a laugh.

Jon Cleary
Author

Jon Stephen Cleary was born in Sydney in 1917. Jon was the eldest of seven children and his family did it tough. 'I remember being ten years old and the debt collectors taking everything from our home except for my mother's bed. Soon after, we lost everything. My dad took five pounds from his employer; instead of getting fired, he was sentenced to six months gaol.' Jon left school just before he turned 15, as his family needed extra money. 'To get paid the dole we had to work. I would go to Randwick Town Hall and get a broom and sweep the streets.'

In 1940 Jon joined the Australian Army; he served in the Middle East and New Guinea. In 1941 he was in Lebanon with an Australian ski group. 'I had no idea how to ski. I got a lesson on Friday and by Sunday we were off. I stopped on what I thought was a ledge, but it was just ice on a bush. I fell 100 feet then slid 200 feet. When I got to the bottom I was unconscious and my hands were filled with spikes. My friend helped me get to a place where they had donkeys. I had to roll in the snow every ten minutes to stop the bleeding. I spent three months in hospital and in February 1942 was on board a ship bound for Australia.'

After the war Jon wanted to become a writer. He intended to make his books as authentic as possible. If he was going to write a book about a remote village on the other side of the world, for example, then he would live there. 'The writers these days just sit on the Internet, look at a photo and write about that place. I was fortunate to travel around the world. You must be somewhere to write about it, otherwise you just don't get the smell or the feel of the place.'

In 1958 Jon and his wife Joy went to New Guinea to write a book. 'We had to trek for three days. We had a police escort, because instead of chiefs they had fight leaders, and after a fight the winner would eat the loser! It was very primitive; my wife was the first white woman they had ever seen, and after the third touch of her breast, she stepped back and said, "If you touch me again I'll kick you inbetween the legs." The translator told the fight leader what she had said and he just stared at her, but after a moment he let out this tremendous laugh, and from that day on she was treated like a queen.'

Jon has written over forty books, but he is most famous for his Scoby Malone character, named after jockey Scobie Breasley. Many of his books have been made into movies, including *The Sundowners*, which he wrote while working as a journalist in New York. 'I would work in the day and write the book at night. I received a phone call from my agent in America telling me that Fred Zimmerman wanted to make *The Sundowners* into a movie.' Jon agreed and also wrote the screenplay for the movie, which starred Robert Mitchum and Deborah Kerr. *The High Commissioner* was another one of his classic books that was made into a movie, this time starring Rod Taylor. 'I was in London and was walking into Australia House and I met a policeman from Australia; we spoke for only five minutes. Then I went inside and pressed the lift button and thought to myself, what if he had come to London to arrest the High Commissioner for murder? And that's how the book and movie started. The *New York Times* said that the opening line of the movie was the best narrative line of the season.'

Jon has had an unbelievably colourful life, fighting bushfires and blizzards in America, falling 300 feet down a cliff in Lebanon and visiting remote towns and villages all around the world. Now in his late eighties, Jon still writes on his 1948 typewriter; a typewriter that has given the world some wonderful literature. Even now after more than 60 years, every new Jon Cleary book is still guaranteed to sell more than 125 000 sales.

I met Jon in 2001 at his apartment in Kirribilli. He was a very warm and intelligent man who gave me much of his time. He is a natural storyteller, and has sold between eight and nine million books worldwide. Yet he remains extremely modest and unpretentious.

Barry Crocker

I'M SURE most of us at one time or another have used or heard the term 'I'm having a Barry Crocker,' meaning 'I'm having a shocker.' Well, Barry Crocker is more than just a catch phrase. He is a singer, actor, writer, producer, TV compere and comedian.

Born Barry Hugh Crocker in the town of Geelong, Victoria in 1935, Barry always aspired to be something special, but at first he just wasn't sure how to get there, or what it was exactly. As a child in kindergarten Barry used to make funny noises—and make the other kids pay to see or hear his unusual talents. The entertaining didn't stop at school, however; young Barry would continue to entertain his family at home with his one-man shows. After a 14-month tour with John Broadway who was a juggler, Barry auditioned for the JC Williamson Company. It was the kind of break Barry had been searching for, but he was not hired by the company because of his height—he was told that he would stand out too much from the crowd.

In 1959 Barry teamed up with fellow entertainer Dave Clark. They toured extensively throughout Australia with their shows, and the names Crocker and Clarke slowly but surely began to make headlines. At this time television was also taking off in Australia and Barry managed to get his own show, called *Sound of Music*, which co-starred fellow entertainer Toni Lamond. The highly successful show ran for five years and won numerous awards. Not content with conquering Australia, Barry then left for overseas. He found success in numerous countries, including Canada, America and England. Barry was now an international star. He returned to Australia to star in the cult film *The Adventures of Barry McKenzie*, written by fellow performer Barry Humphries and directed by Bruce Beresford. The movie broke box office records both here and in the United Kingdom.

Between 1969-1970 Barry won four Logie Awards: two for best male artist and two for best variety artist. He also won a best national variety show award. Barry kept releasing numerous albums and performing. He worked overseas, including a hit four-week season at the famed MGM Grand Hotel in Las Vegas. He also worked in the United States on a number of television shows.

Barry has divided his time between Australia, the United States and Britain, performing in variety shows, cabaret shows and recording hit albums (he has over 30 gold records). He has hosted the British television show *Saturday Variety*. He has also hosted and appeared in numerous Australian television shows including *In Melbourne Tonight* and *Punishment* (the male version of *Prisoner*). In 1985 Barry recorded the original theme song for the hit soapie *Neighbours*. This allowed a new generation and audience to enjoy his many talents. The producers used his version from 1985 to 1992.

In 1980 *This is Your Life* covered Barry's life—he continues to work; he does cabaret and television spots, has performed in another musical, the all-Australian themed extravaganza *Eureka*, in which he plays Paddy O'Malley, and in 2003 he released his autobiography, *Bazza*.

I literally bumped into Barry Crocker in Sydney's Martin Place in 2000. Barry was preparing for a show, to raise money for charity. I took my chance and asked him for a quick photo shoot 'on the spot' for this book and exhibition. He graciously and happily agreed. I took a roll of photographs. He thanked me and then said, 'I've got to run and raise some money for the kids'. He left to do what he does best ... entertain the crowd.

Bart Cummings

Horse trainer

THE MELBOURNE Cup is the race that stops the nation; every year millions of Australians place a bet on the race. Bart Cummings, on the other hand not only hopes for a win but is expected to win. This may seem a bit extreme, but considering Bart Cummings has won the Melbourne Cup eleven times (as a trainer)—a record that most probably will never be beaten—it is a reality.

Born James Bartholomew Cummings in Adelaide on 14 November 1927, Bart grew up surrounded by horses. His father, Jim Cummings, was a horse trainer who won the Melbourne Cup in 1950—in race record time—in front of 81 000 people at Flemington.

In 1953 Bart was working as a stable foreman at his father's stables. His father was travelling in Ireland for six months so Bart had to get a licence to train the horses while his father was away.

'I started training horses when I was young. The ones I was originally given were almost impossible to win with, so I went to yearling sales and picked the ones that I thought looked like race horses; this gave me an even break to win and compete with other trainers.'

Bart obviously had a natural eye for picking a winner and the talent to train a good horse into a champion. In 1958 Bart purchased his first yearling and that same year he won the South Australian Derby. However, everything was about to change. In 1965 Bart won his first Melbourne Cup with Light Fingers. 'It was a tremendous feeling winning my first Melbourne Cup,' he remembers.

The 1965-66 racing season turned Bart Cummings into a legend overnight. He took out his first trainers' premiership with seven cup wins: he had won the quinella on the Melbourne Cup and Adelaide Cup, plus the Caulfield, Sandown, Sydney, Brisbane and Queens Cups. The following year, in 1967, Bart won his third (consecutive) Melbourne Cup. He continued to win major races, and in 1968 moved from Adelaide to Sydney.

In 1974 Bart won another Melbourne Cup with Think Big. In that same year, Bart became the first trainer to win one million dollars in prize money in a single season from his winning horses. The next year, 1975, was a great year for Bart. He moved to Leilani Lodge at Randwick Racecourse, won the Melbourne Cup and was named ABC Sportsman of the Year. Bart also won the Melbourne Cup in 1977, 1979, 1990, 1991, 1996 and in 1999 (for the eleventh time) with Rogan Josh.

It was his win with Saintly in 1996 that Bart considers his most notable achievement: 'Saintly won the Melbourne Cup and the Cox Plate—it's a rare double. I was the trainer, part-owner and breeder; that win put the icing on the cake.'

Winning 11 Melbourne Cups is an amazing achievement, but Bart is not content. 'I want to win for the twelfth time—nothing like a baker's dozen!' says Bart with a laugh. Bart Cummings is not just 'The King' of the Melbourne Cup; he has won more than double of his nearest rival trainer in group one winners. With those statistics he is definitely the Bradman of horse training.

In the 1989-90 racing season Bart was the first trainer to win premierships in three different states (South Australia, Victoria and New South Wales). In 2004 the Victorian Racing Committee named the inaugural running of The Bart Cummings Race, which is a $100 000, 2500 metre handicap race in honour of Cummings.

I met Bart Cummings in November 2004 at his Randwick stables. When I asked him if he feels any pressure every year to win the Melbourne Cup, he gave me a smirk and pointed to a cartoon that hangs in his office. It's of an elderly couple speaking to another elderly person with the caption: 'My Len never forgets when we married: it was the year Bart didn't win the cup'. Bart had a good laugh at the cartoon and gave me plenty of time to take my photos and do an interview.

Sir Roden Cutler

ARTHUR RODEN Cutler was born on 24 May 1916 in the northern Sydney beachside suburb of Manly. Roden was given his maternal grandmother's maiden name. After completing his schooling at Sydney Boys High School, he enrolled at Sydney University, where he joined the regiment to earn extra money. On 10 November 1939, he was commissioned as a lieutenant in the military. When World War II broke out he joined the second Australian Imperial Force (AIF) as a lieutenant in the 2/5th Field Regiment of the 7th Division artillery. He and his unit left Australia on 20 October 1940 to fight in the Middle East.

From 19 June to 6 July 1941, near the town of Merdjayoun, Syria, the Australians were under attack by tanks and heavy machine-gun fire. Aged only twenty-five, Cutler and a small group of men continued to push forward and eventually established an outpost in a house. The enemy were relentlessly attacking the house, but Cutler and the other men continued to fight and eventually the enemy withdrew. Cutler continued to push forward into enemy territory; once again the enemy attacked, using infantry and tanks. Roden, now separated from the group, was forced to make his way back to base in the darkness of the night. Because of his determination to continue to fight, the enemy eventually retreated and Merdjayoun was recaptured by the Allies.

At Damour, Cutler once again put his life on the line when the infantry's wireless would not work. In the mountainous countryside, Cutler carried a telephone line through the enemy's occupied area so he could bring artillery fire down. Cutler was able to capture eight Frenchmen but was under constant fire. He was eventually shot in the right leg and lay in the fields in an enormous amount of pain for 26 hours, before he was found by one of his men. Roden's injury became gangrenous and as a result his right leg was amputated just above his knee. For this reason Cutler had to return to Australia.

On his return home he heard on the BBC radio that he was to be awarded the Victoria Cross, an honour he was awarded on 11 June 1942 for his tremendous bravery. After the war Cutler became a high commissioner, minister, secretary-general, consul-general and an ambassador to numerous countries. In 1946 he married Helen Morris; they had four sons and were together until her death in 1990. Sir Roden remarried in 1993.

In 1963 he was knighted by Queen Elizabeth II and the following year in 1966 Roden became Governor of NSW. He was to become the state's longest-serving governor, retiring in 1981 after fifteen years of service. In 2000, Sir Roden, along with two other Victoria Cross winners, was honoured by Australia Post in a release of 'For Valour' stamps to commemorate their heroic achievements.

My first experience of Sir Roden came when I was only 17: at the Anzac Day march in 1990. I was walking around taking photos when I saw a mother dragging her young child through the crowds saying to her child, 'Can you see him? That's the great Roden Cutler!' Her child, who was only about seven, could not see Sir Roden through the crowds. The mother and child continued their chase through the crowd, and out of curiosity I followed. Sir Roden's car finally pulled to the side of the road and the mother and child, puffing and panting, waited for him to exit his vehicle. When he did the lady said, 'I've always admired you and I just wanted to thank you for everything you did for our country.' Sir Roden, as down-to-earth and modest as anyone that I have ever met, held his hand out and thanked the lady for her kind words.

I was blessed to meet Sir Roden a few times at his house in Sydney and found him to be extremely kind, and generous with his time. He was a humble man who had to learn to accept his greatness. Sir Roden Cutler passed away on 21 February 2002 and is truly missed by people throughout the world. Sir Roden was a hero but he was also a people person, with an uncanny gift to unite people from all walks of life.

Sir William Dargie

Artist

WILLIAM ALEXANDER DARGIE was born on 4 June 1912 at Footscray in Victoria. His mother Mary, who he idolised, was a schoolteacher and wanted her son to have a good education. This is the main reason why, after Dargie finished school, he completed a teacher training course and became a full-time teacher.

In 1931 a friend took William to meet Melbourne artist Archie Colquhoun. William wandered around Colquhoun's studio and decided that he wanted to paint. He then took a year's unpaid leave from teaching and studied art, hanging around Colquhoun's studio, as well as studying part-time at Melbourne Technical College. After a year learning the skills of an artist, Dargie returned to teaching at school: 'I taught a lot of people. I liked teaching.'

By 1936 William had started painting portraits and landscapes, but he seemed to be a natural at portraiture. During this period he met his wife Kathleen and they married in 1937. 'She was a very good artist as well and understood what it took to become an artist.' In 1941 William served in World War II as a war artist, before leaving Australia he painted a portrait of Sir James Elder. It was this painting that won William his first Archibald Prize. 'I was in the south of Tobruk digging a trench, and this friend of mine came over and said to me, "I've got this letter for you. What is it?" I said, "It's from my wife—I've won the Archibald Prize. "What's that?" he asked. I told him it was for painting portraits. I didn't react at all strangely enough. How could I? I was at war!'

William won the Archibald Prize a total of eight times: in 1941 then 1942, 1945, 1946, 1947, 1950, 1952, and his last in 1956, with a painting of fellow artist Albert Namatjira. Dargie's dominance of the Archibald Prize saw him being denounced by other artists and art critics. In 1952, after Dargie had won his seventh Archibald, a group of Sydney art students headed by a then unknown 24-year old John Olsen vigorously protested against the judges' decision. Olsen and other art students held up signs in the gallery such as: 'Art ain't just paint', 'Archibald decision death to art' and 'Winner of the Archibald Prize William Doggie'.

After William won his eighth Archibald, fellow artist and art critic James Gleeson wrote: 'How threadbare can a tradition become before it finally dissolves into thin air? It is his eighth victory and that in itself is a sad commentary on the wretched condition of portrait painting in this country.'

William continued to paint throughout his entire life and was an official artist to the Queen, painting her portrait three times. William was also a successful businessman, creating the first television production house in Australia.

I met Sir William on two occasions and had a few telephone conversations with him between 2000 and 2003. I found out that he didn't see himself first and foremost as an artist, but considered himself a businessman who had a talent for painting portraits. My last conversation with Sir William, just before he died was in relation to an article that he had read about himself. He told me that he felt greatly depressed that people were still questioning his Archibald achievements. 'After all the fuss and bother it all caused [winning the Archibald so many times], I'll tell you I would have been inhuman to be silly enough to carry on entering the Archibald, it was as if I had done something terrible.' It's amazing that our greatest portrait painter felt that he shouldn't be thought of as an artist. Or maybe it was just the jealousy and egos of other artists that kept Dargie from considering himself Australia's greatest portrait painter.

Smoky Dawson

Country singer

SMOKEY DAWSON was born Herbert Henry Dawson on 19 March 1913 in Victoria. Herbert's father was an entertainer; unfortunately, his father was also an alcoholic and would beat Herbert daily. His mother died when he was six, and when he was eight he ran away from home and sold newspapers to survive. Herbert was finally picked up by a welfare agency and placed into St Vincent de Paul's orphanage. During his time there, Herbert sang in the choir. 'They found out I had a good voice and I became the leading voice in the choir.' During his time in the orphanage Smoky won prizes for his writing and composition.

After three years in the orphanage he ran away and ended up in Ned Kelly country (in the north east of Victoria). He then started working on farms, where he learnt country songs and how to play the harmonica.

It was around this time that young Herbie became known as Smoky: 'Peter Ryan, who was a friend of the Kellys, offered me a puff on his pipe; I took one big puff and coughed until I was nearly unconscious. Word got around town and the locals would say, "How's the smoke today?" People around town eventually started calling me Smoky.'

Smoky and his brother formed a band and would play at local parties and other events, under the name of the Coral Island Boys. They eventually made a demo and the director of Fidelity Records heard the song and gave it to 3KZ radio. 'The guy at the radio station said to me, "We need a name for you," so I said Smoky. From that day in 1935 I was known as Smoky Dawson.'

Dawson broadcast country music on 3KZ and was the first Australian artist on radio to replace an American program. It was during this time at the station that Smoky met Florence (Dot) Cheers and her sister Jean, who were also performers. Dot is the love of Smoky's life; they married in 1944 and to this day he still writes love songs for her, after 60 glorious years of marriage. 'Dot was the only one and I still hold her hand everywhere we go.'

Smoky signed with Columbia Records in 1941 and began to tour Australia. However, Smoky's tours were not your usual show. Smoky was a cowboy and his shows included singing, playing guitar, animal noises, knife and axe-throwing, horse-riding, whip-cracking and storytelling. During the 1940s and 1950s, Australian children were obsessed with American cowboys; with Smoky Dawson they had their very own. Instead of watching cowboys at the movies, people could now watch Smoky do his travelling show all around Australia. He could throw a knife or axe from 20 feet, and he never once hit or injured a person. Smoky had learnt his skills during the war when he was sent to Borneo and learnt to throw, practising with bayonets.

In 1951 Smoky and Dot travelled to the United States and performed all over the country; Smoky was now an international cowboy. 'When I toured America I took a kangaroo with me. I did shows with Hank Williams and all the biggies. I took my knives and axes and did my show all over. One day we were heading to the Roxy Theatre in a cadillac and the kangaroo jumped out of the car. It was lost for five days in New York and it made front page news in all of the New York papers. It was eventually found asleep in a park under a tree!' To this very day Smoky is idolised in Nashville, Tennessee.

Smoky returned home a huge star and in 1952 the Smoky Dawson radio show went on air. Almost every child in Australia was a member of the Smoky Dawson Wild West club. This is inconceivable in today's world. Even a very young deputy sheriff by the name of Paul Keating was proud to call Smoky his idol.

Smoky continued to perform his wild west shows for many years and today, at 91, he has just signed a new record deal.

Smoky Dawson is a natural storyteller, a compassionate man and a real cowboy. When I last visited Smoky in 2004, he sung two new love songs that he had written for his wife and told me amazing stories about being Australia's first cowboy.

John Dowie

Sculptor/artist

JOHN STUART DOWIE was born on 15 January 1915 in Adelaide. He attended the Rose Park Primary School. When he was just ten he started to draw and create sculptures from wax. A friend of his sister told his father that young John had considerable talent, and in 1925, at the age of ten, he began modelling and drawing classes at the South Australian School of Art.

After completing high school in 1932, John started work as a clerk, but it was the arts that excited him. In 1936 John studied architecture at the University of Adelaide, as well as studying part-time at the South Australian Art School. But like many people born before 1920, World War II interrupted his life. John enlisted in the military in 1940. In 1941 he left Australia, serving in Luxor, the famous siege of Tobruk, and Palestine. John was also an assistant (for six months) to an Australian sculptor who was an official war artist for the Australian war memorial.

In 1945 John left the army. He continued to paint and sculpt and studied under Ivor Hele at the South Australian School of Art. John's paintings were full of colour and humour and his sculptures were creative, while being extremely accurate. In 1950 John left Australia for London. He spent some time travelling to Norway and Sweden to see for himself the works of renowned sculptors Gustav Vgeland and Carl Milles. He then returned to his base in London. John studied at the Sir John Cass College in London as a stone sculptor; he then studied bronze casting at Porta Romania College and sculpture modelling at The Academia in Florence. John spent three years studying and travelling throughout Europe, and in 1953 returned to Adelaide, where he took a teaching position at the South Australian School of Art. Three years' worth of his paintings and sculptures—the ones created overseas—were disastrously lost in transit during the return trip home to Australia.

Soon after his arrival back in Australia, John began to get commissions to do sculptures. His first was for the Roseworthy Campus of the University of Adelaide. Then in 1957 he created a sculpture of aviator Sir Ross Smith for Adelaide Airport; this opened the door to other commissions. In 1959 John sculpted the face of famed climber Sir Edmund Hilary. 'Ed Hilary was one of the good people to meet. It was the fastest sculpture I've ever done. He sat for me for one hour, and then I was lucky to get one more hour out of him. As time went on John sculpted many more famous people, from Sir Marcus Oliphant to Lloyd Rees, and in 1987 was commissioned by Parliament House to do a full-length sculpture of Queen Elizabeth II for the new Parliament House in Canberra.

'I arrived at Buckingham Palace and was supposed to meet a gentleman but he didn't turn up. Another man replaced him and told me the Queen was running late. I was in a bit of a fluster, then all of a sudden the Queen walks into the room. She noticed that I was a bit flustered, so she made me more comfortable by having fun. We laughed and had fun for the entire sitting. She was a very humorous and intelligent woman; she was marvellous.' The sculpture of Queen Elizabeth II was so good that Buckingham Palace requested another to be made for their private collection. John's works can be seen all over Australia, particularly in Adelaide, where it seems John has designed the city. His sculptures are everywhere. The most famous is the Three Rivers Fountain in Victoria Square, which he created in 1968.

Now 90, John has been sculpting and painting for 80 years. When I met him in 2004, he was busy working in his studio with the enthusiasm and energy of a 20-year-old. 'You've got to keep working, keep creating, never stop!' he told me with excitement. Though he realises he is known for his sculptures he would like to be remembered for both his painting and sculptures. John is a generous and affectionate man, with an insatiable giggle. Even though he has been clearly influenced by his travels overseas, he has ultimately chosen to live and work in South Australia in his childhood home, where he still lives.

Robert Dunford

ROBERT DUNFORD was born on 25 November 1898. Like most young Australian boys at the time he enlisted in the Australian Army, joining in April 1918 as a nineteen-year-old. At the time he was working as a farm labourer at Currabubula, NSW. Dunford was a gunner with the 1st Division Ammunition Column. He left Australia on the HMTS *Feldmarschall* to train in England, and arrived in August that year. 'When we left Australia the war had been going on for some time. We didn't sign up for the excitement, we signed up because we had to—the Australian Army needed more men. On the journey to Southhampton there was a bit of trouble. The boat was crowded and they wouldn't let any of the troops sleep on the top deck. There was no room on the boat, so some of the men decided to sleep on the deck. It got so bad that the captain threatened to bring in another battalion of the Australian Army, but it backfired, because one Australian wouldn't shoot another. So in the end we won—half the boys slept on the deck and the other half slept on hammocks down below.

Robert trained at Salisbury Plain and then went to France to fight in the war as a gunner. During his time in England and France Robert also trained in gas and trench warfare. When he arrived in France in 1918 World War I was officially over. 'Just as we arrived Armistice was being signed, so we didn't see any action. I guess I was lucky.'

However, Robert and the other servicemen who arrived in France were given the gruesome task of cleaning up the cities, towns, streets and buildings that had been destroyed. They had a very tough time rebuilding man-made buildings and entire communities—not only were structures destroyed; so too were the spirits of the men, women and children whose lives had been irreversibly changed. Though Dunford never saw any action during World War I, he played a pivotal role by cleaning up the battlefields on the Western Front in France and Belgium.

'When we arrived it was a mess. We spent the whole time over there cleaning up. It was rugged, rough and tough. Buildings were everywhere and thousands of people had been killed; I remember every day of that time.'

Robert returned to Australia in October 1919 and worked as a dairy farmer, and then studied accountancy. In later life Robert and his wife Thelma ran a newsagency. In May 2000 Robert Dunford was presented with the 80th Anniversary Armistice Remembrance Medal. In 2002 he was also awarded the Centenary Medal, these were given to all Australians who were alive at the time of Federation in 1901.

On 7 May 2003 I went with a friend to Robert Dunford's nursing home. I had had the address for over two years, but for some reason had never been able to visit him. On 7 May I had a very strong urge to visit Dunford. We arrived at the nursing home just after lunch and met Robert and his friend. I was told that he had not been well the previous day but was in good spirits this particular day. I took the photos and interviewed him. He was a warm and cheerful man, and like most World War I veterans, was very modest and did not see what all the fuss was about. However, he did think that it was important that schoolchildren learnt about the sacrifices that all those men and women made during the wars, and to pass on the legacy.

My friend and I left the nursing home at about 3.30 pm. At 6.00 pm I received a phone call informing me that after we had left Robert had been in a great mood. He'd had a glass of whisky then passed away in his sleep.

Jack Dyer

Football player/commentator

BORN JOHN RAYMOND DYER in Melbourne in 1913, Jack attended St Ignatius School and later De La Salle College, in Malvern.

In May 1931, Jack was named nineteenth man in the Richmond first-grade VFL side; Jack demonstrated enormous passion in his playing. His size, skill and determination ensured that he was later named in Richmond's first-grade side of that year. Jack was to play 312 games for the Richmond Tigers; his career lasted from 1931 to 1949 and in his last game he kicked six goals. He captained Victoria in 1941 and 1949. He kicked 443 goals for the Tigers and won best and fairest six times, which is ironic, because he is known by many fans as Captain Blood (the name of a film character played by Errol Flynn). This nickname was given to him after a game in 1935 against Fitzroy (now the Brisbane Lions) where he crumbled three players. Dyer was regarded as the toughest ruckman to play the game. But he was a highly-skilled player; he had high speed and also a very precise kick.

Jack Dyer was a born leader who always led his men with courage and passion. Never one to be intimidated by the opposition, Jack played the game rough and tough like no other player before him. He once broke the collarbones of five opposition players in one season, but throughout his entire playing career, Jack was only suspended once.

Like many great sportsmen, Jack was loved by the Tiger fans and hated by the opposition's fans. In one game Jack knocked out an opposition player and the fans of the opposition side had had enough. After the game more than two hundred angry fans waited for Jack to leave the sportsground. Jack was also a policeman, and when he emerged from the ground he was dressed in his police uniform. He raised his gun into the air and ran to his car, which was pelted with rocks and bottles.

The great Lou Richards tells of an incident when he was playing against Captain Blood: Richards jumped up behind Jack to take a mark and in the process 'accidentally' hit Jack in the ear. Jack turned around and clipped Richards behind the ear, telling him to pick on somebody his own size. Richards learnt a valuable lesson from that encounter; if he couldn't hack it, he should pick up his school bag and go home.

After coaching the club from 1941 until 1952 in 225 games, Jack finally retired from his football and coaching duties and began a career in the media—concentrating on television and the radio. This career lasted over 20 years. He became a much-loved personality in the AFL-playing states, especially in his home town of Melbourne.

While I was in Melbourne my friend looked over my list of names and said, 'You don't have Captain Blood. He is the greatest VFL player still alive; he is a living legend and you have to get him!' Coming from Sydney, I had not heard of Jack 'Captain Blood' Dyer before, but I was about to embark on that journey.

In December 2002 I arrived at Jack's nursing home just after lunch and went into meet him. He was 89 years of age and still had an amazing sense of humour; he was always laughing and joking throughout the photoshoot. He told my friend and I that we had brightened up his day. Jack 'Captain Blood' Dyer passed away on 23 August 2003.

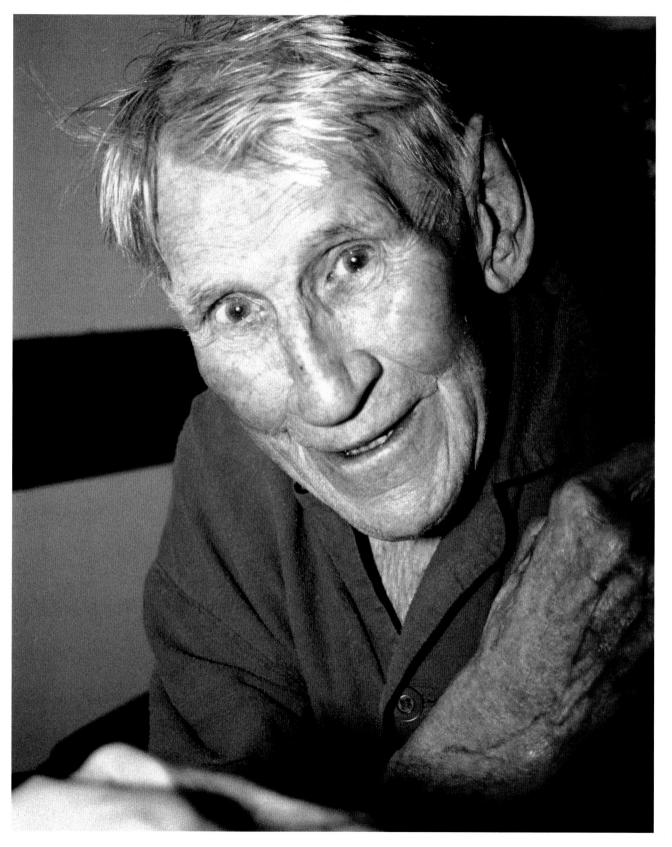

Herb Elliot

Athlete

MOST 22-YEAR OLDS are still trying to work out what they are going to choose as a career. For Herb Elliot, at 22, he had already retired from athletic competition.

Herb was born on 25 February 1938 in Perth. From an early age he showed tremendous skill as a middle distance runner and at just 14 he had run his first mile race, in 5 minutes and 35 seconds. Two years later at 16, he won the schoolboy mile in 4:25.6 secs. The time was considered a world record time for his age group. That same year Herb competed in an open athletic competition in Perth. He entered the 100, 220, 440 and 880 yards dashes and won all of them. To top it off, he won the mile and the broad jump as well. In 1956 Herb watched the Olympic Games in Melbourne; this inspired him to compete at the next Olympic Games which were to be held in Rome in 1960.

Herb joined Percy Cerutty's training camp. Cerutty was well known for pushing people to their limits and his new pupil did not get any favours. Herb trained extremely hard, running hours every day. He practised on the track, and he and his coach would run in the sand dunes at Cerutty's Portsea training camp. His training with Cerutty was crucial in terms of Herb's mental and physical preparation for the track. To this day Herb says that he wouldn't have been able to achieve all he did without Cerutty's diligence and support.

In 1957 Herb won the Australian Mile Championship and in January of 1958 he ran his first mile in under 4 minutes. That year proved to be a good year for Herb: he represented Australia at the Empire Games (Commonwealth Games) in Cardiff, winning gold in the mile and the 880 yards, then one month later in Dublin he ran the fastest mile in the world (3:54.5), becoming the youngest athlete to break the 4 minute mile, taking an astonishing 2.7 seconds off the previous record. Herb then broke the world record for the 1500 metres in Sweden, knocking 2.1 seconds off the record. Herb had become an international star in athletics and was also voted American Sportsman of the year.

He was offered a staggering $250 000 by an American entrepreneur to turn professional; all of this and more in one year. Herb turned down the money because he wanted to represent Australia at the 1960 Rome Olympics. At this early stage of his life Herb had won everything except an Olympic medal.

In 1959 Herb took a break from his gruelling training schedule. He went to Melbourne University, got married and tried to focus on other sides of his life, but as the 1960 Olympic Games drew closer, Herb knew he had to get back into full-time training. He ran an average of 90 kilometres per week, and did weight training and sprints as well.

All the hard work paid off in the 1960 Rome Olympics, when Herb ran the race of his life, winning the 1500 metres and in doing so breaking his own world record. His nearest opponent was more than 20 metres behind him.

Herb was now an Olympic champion. He was content with his gold medal and world record, and retired from competitive athletics in 1961. Herb was an undefeated champion throughout his short but brilliant athletics career. Herb was such a natural athlete that he only ever lost one mile race: it was as a junior and to a competitor who was three years his senior.

In 2000, I met and photographed Herb Elliot in his Sydney office, when he was working for the Australian Olympic Committee. After a few photos, I thought that a simple office photo may be a little boring, so I asked Herb if he had anything that might add to the photograph. The only thing he had was a pair of ladies running shoes, which I asked him to pretend to put on. The expression on his face was priceless—we both summed up the moment with a good hearty laugh.

Johnny Famechon

Boxer

JOHNNY FAMECHON was born in France on 28 March 1945. The Famechon family moved to Australia when Johnny was just five. At 11, Johnny's father bought him his first pair of boxing gloves; not to use in fighting but to develop himself physically. His father thought that Johnny was too fragile to fight. A few years later Famechon showed a great interest in boxing. His father, who had been a boxing champion in France, took his son to Ambrose Palmer's gym. Ambrose took one look at the small-framed kid and told him to come back later, when he had grown a bit more. A few days passed and Johnny returned to the gym and showed off his boxing skills to Ambrose. Ambrose quickly recognised Johnny's talent, noting that he had natural speed in the ring. Palmer placed Johnny on a strict regime, training him to produce quick bursts of speed and then recover quickly. Johnny was taught to protect himself: 'I always had my guard up,' he recalls.

After some time training with Palmer, Johnny was ready for his first professional fight; this made him a rarity as he had never boxed as an amateur. In 1961, Johnny had his first professional fight. It ended in a three-round draw, but this short fight was just the beginning of a wonderful career. In 1964 Johnny defeated Les Dunn for the Victorian Featherweight title, and on 18 September that year he won the Australian Featherweight title. In 1967 he defeated Scot Johnny O'Brien for the Empire Featherweight title. With 58 fights under his belt, Johnny was ready for an attempt at a world title.

On 21 January 1969 Johnny took on Cuban boxer Jose Legra for the World Featherweight title. The fight was held in Albert Hall in London. Johnny was not expected to win against the hard-hitting Legra, but he and his coach had a plan. Legra thought of himself as a leaner Muhammad Ali; he had great speed and the ability to knock out his opponents. Johnny's plan was to concentrate on getting close to Legra and throw quick but effective punches into Legra's body. By the final round, Legra had tired and was starting to throw desperate punches at Johnny, who stayed in control. Johnny went on the attack and landed enough blows to take out the fight on points. Johnny became the World Featherweight Champion.

On 28 July 1969, only six months after winning the championship, Johnny defended his title in Sydney, winning a controversial fight against 'Fighting' Harada of Japan. Johnny concentrated almost entirely on defence, and with his brilliant reflexes was able to prevent many of the blows from connecting. However, the crowd wanted to see more of a battling clash, and when Johnny won by only one point the crowd yelled out their disapproval. Six months later, on 6 January 1970, Johnny fought Harada again, in Tokyo, giving the fans what they wanted. Johnny won the fight in a 14-round knockout.

Just four months later, on 9 May 1971 in Rome, he lost the title—a point's decision—to Vicenti Saldivar of Mexico. He and his trainer thought he had won but it was not to be. Characteristically, Johnny just shrugged his shoulders. The very next day he announced his retirement, at only 25 years of age.

Johnny was a defensive, quick-moving and elegant fighter. He was not a brutal fighter, but he was thought of by many as a genius in the ring. He was calculating, with sharp skills. This is displayed in his statistics: in his career he only lost five of his 67 fights—all of them by points and never inside the distance. Johnny is the only featherweight champion never to have been knocked out.

In 1991, Johnny was hit by a car while he was jogging; many believed that he was not going to pull through, but his determination and perseverance once again paid off. However, his severe injuries left him brain-damaged. Like a true champion, though, he is still fighting.

When I met Johnny in 1999 we spent the whole time laughing. He has not lost any of his personality; he was positive, down-to-earth and always had a tongue-in-cheek story to tell. Johnny Famechon is a true champion and an inspiration to us all, in and out of the ring.

Dawn Fraser

Swimmer

In DAWN FRASER's nine-year swimming career she set 39 (27 individual) world records and won eight Olympic medals. From 1956 to 1964 she won the 110 yards freestyle event at the Australian championships seven times, and the 220 yards freestyle eight times. She is one of the world's greatest swimmers of all time. Not bad for a girl from Sydney who started swimming as a child to help with her asthma.

Dawn Fraser is a swimming champion who is never afraid to tell it like it is. Born on 4 September 1937, Fraser was the youngest of eight children. She was persuaded to swim by her brother Don, who would accompany her to the pool. Sadly, Don died when Dawn was just 13. But Dawn wanted to keep her brother's dream alive, so she continued to swim, and when she was 16, swimming coach Harry Gallagher noticed her aptitude in the water and began coaching her for free. Dawn became a strong and determined swimmer, training against male swimmers.

In 1956 Dawn competed in the Olympic Games, which were held in Melbourne.

She won a gold medal in the 110 yards freestyle. In this race she set a new world and Olympic Games record. Dawn backed up her win four years later at the 1960 Rome Olympic Games by winning gold in the 100 metres freestyle. Fraser continued to dominate in the pool by winning four gold medals in the 1962 Commonwealth Games. It was here, on 24 November 1962, that Dawn became the first woman to swim 100 metres freestyle in less than a minute. It would be another ten years before her record would be broken by another Aussie swimming sensation, Shane Gould, at the Munich Olympic Games in 1972.

In 1964, before the Tokyo Olympic Games, Dawn's life changed forever. Dawn's mum died in a tragic car accident, which also paralysed Dawn's neck and spine. As a result of these incidents Dawn almost gave up swimming. But she didn't. Remarkably she was still able to win the gold in the 100 metres freestyle at the Tokyo Games. She had now won gold in the same event at three consecutive Games—Melbourne, Rome and Tokyo.

Dawn was the first swimmer to do this. Dawn should've been on top of the world, but she was wrongly accused of climbing a flagpole at Emperor Hirohito's Palace and taking the Olympic flag.

The Australian swimming union banned Fraser from competitive swimming for ten years. The ban was eventually lifted after four years, but because of the ban Dawn missed the 1968 Mexico Olympic Games. Many believe that if she had not been banned she would've won four consecutive Olympic gold medals in the same event; especially because the winning time in Mexico was .5 seconds slower than Dawn's time at Tokyo. Ironically, in 1964 Dawn was named Australian of the Year. In 1965 she retired from competitive swimming.

Life after swimming was just as busy for Fraser; she married, had a daughter and began to coach. She also worked in a pub in her beloved suburb of Balmain, and in 1988 was elected to represent Balmain in the NSW Parliament.

Dawn has been given many prominent awards over the years, and in 1988 she was voted Australia's greatest female athlete. She was also named Australian Female Athlete of the Century and the World's Greatest Living Female Water Sports Champion, by the IOC (International Olympic Committee) in 1999.

In 2000, at the Sydney Olympic Opening Ceremony, Fraser was an Olympic torchbearer. Fraser continues to live in her much-loved Balmain and remains very independent in her thoughts on swimming today.

In 1996 Hollywood legend Esther Williams came to Sydney for a benefit luncheon in honour of Dawn. I photographed Dawn and Esther on the replica *Bounty* ship at The Rocks in Sydney. Williams told me that the photo summed up her time in Sydney and the friendship that she had with Fraser, and asked for a copy. It was a great thrill for me to meet two legends at once and be lucky enough to capture that moment.

Malcolm Fraser

Former prime minister

JOHN MALCOLM FRASER was born in Victoria on 21 May 1930. He attended Geelong Preparatory School, Tudor House in Sydney, then, back to Victoria, finished his schooling at Melbourne Grammar. Fraser studied philosophy, politics and economics at Oxford University in the United Kingdom. He graduated with a degree in all three subjects. After returning from the United Kingdom, he worked as a grazier; but it was politics that interested him.

In 1954 Fraser contested the Federal seat of Wannon as the Liberal candidate, but was unsuccessful. The following year at just twenty-five years of age, Fraser won the seat, becoming the youngest member in Federal Parliament. He held this seat for twenty-nine years, winning eleven general elections. It wasn't until 31 March 1983 that Fraser gave up his seat to retire. Under Sir John Gorton's leadership Fraser was the Minister for Army, Education and Science. From 1969 to 1971 Fraser was Minister for Defence. On 8 March 1971, Fraser resigned from his position, claiming Gorton had been disloyal to him over army issues. On 22 March 1971 William McMahon successfully challenged Gorton's leadership and became Australia's prime minister.

On 5 December 1972 Gough Whitlam defeated William McMahon in the federal election and became prime minister. On 21 March 1975 Fraser became leader of the Opposition—a move that would change Australian politics forever. On 15 October 1975, Fraser set the wheels in motion to dismiss Gough Whitlam's government. Fraser claimed that Whitlam's Government tried to evade the Loans Council by acquiring funds from overseas, which constituted 'extraordinary and reprehensible circumstances'. Fraser demanded an election. Whitlam, who was also a strong-minded individual, refused Fraser's demands. In turn, Fraser would not pass Budget Bills through the Senate, which postponed the financial support of the government's operations. Fraser stated that the Opposition would not consent to deliver the Budget until the Whitlam government called a general election. The Australian Government was in a deadlock: neither Whitlam nor Fraser would budge. On 11 November 1975 the Governor-General, JR Kerr, rescinded Whitlam's appointment as prime minister and appointed Fraser as a 'stand-in' prime minister until the electon was held.

On 13 December 1975 Fraser's party, with the Country Party, won government in a landslide and Fraser became the new prime minister. The Whitlam/Fraser controversy would be the most talked about political event in the history of Australian politics. Fraser served as our prime minister from 13 December 1975 until he was defeated by Bob Hawke on 6 March 1983. Fraser resigned from Parliament on 11 March 1983.

During his time as prime minister, Fraser enacted various new pieces of legislation. In 1976 the Aboriginal Land Rights (Northern Territory) Act gave land rights to Northern Territory Aborigines—and in 1980 the Aboriginal Development Commission Act, which gave funding for Aboriginal enterprises, housing and other related services, was passed.

In 1981 his government declared 36 000 square metres of Cairns' Great Barrier Reef as a marine park. The Australian land and sea were obviously very important to Fraser. After politics he focused on caring for those in need. He became the head of Care Australia, which, among other things, provides help to poverty-afflicted countries in Africa.

I met Malcolm Fraser in 2002 at his office in Melbourne. After I did the photo shoot, I packed up my gear, which included my camera equipment plus some folders. About 15 minutes later I received a phone call from his secretary asking if I had packed up one of Mr Fraser's folders from his desk. I looked at my own folders and noticed that I had. Thinking I had a folder that contained documents about national security, I quickly rushed back to Fraser's office, puffing and in a slight panic, only to be told that it was a folder containing information about his favourite dogs!

James Gleeson

Artist

SURREALISM IS A MOVEMENT in art and literature emphasising expression of the unconscious. James Gleeson is Australia's best-known surrealist painter. Born on 21 November 1915 in Sydney, Gleeson's father died in a flu epidemic when James was a child, so the family moved to Gosford, where his extended family lived. His entire schooling was at Gosford Public School, where he became interested in art. His aunt taught him how to paint with oils and James decided that he wanted to become an artist. His influences were El Greco, because of his ragged skies and threatening atmosphere, then Blake's poetic dreams, and Picasso's destruction of form and rearrangement of it in different ways. But it was Salvador Dali who Gleeson really connected with.

In 1934 James began his studies at the East Sydney Technical College. He was there for two years, and then spent another two years at Sydney Teachers College, where he studied Freud and Jung. It was during this time at the Sydney Teachers College that Gleeson exhibited his first painting, *City of a Tongue*. During the early to mid-1940s, James taught art at Kogarah Girls High School and lectured at Sydney Teachers College, as well as exhibiting his surrealist art. His art shocked the public and the contemporary Australian art scene. 'The papers described my art as child-frightening. People were afraid of surrealism, but people aren't afraid of it anymore, due to TV and movies.'

In the late 1940s, James took a trip to Europe. 'It's only when you see the original art work that you can make contact with the art, nothing compares to the original.' At one stage James and his friends ended up at Salvador Dali's house, but to their disappointment he was not home. However, James was able to meet Peggy Guggenheim, who introduced him to Jackson Pollock's works. James's interest in Pollock's work would later see him in hot water. On his return home from Europe, James became an art critic for the *Sun* newspaper and later for the *Sun Herald*. He continued to paint, to travel to Europe and America and exhibit throughout Australia.

Between 1955 and 1960 he combined surrealist paintings with perfect sculptured humans, giving his unreal world a sense of distorted realism. By placing humans in his work he was aiming to create a sense of immortality, and worship of the body. James was now spending more time being an art critic and researching and writing books on art. Writing engaged him almost as much as painting and in the process he gained great respect as an art historian.

In 1974 James became chairman of the acquisitions committee at the Australian National Gallery. It was during this time that he was offered Jackson Pollock's *Blue Poles* for the gallery. *Blue Poles* was Pollock's masterpiece and an opportunity that James could not pass up. He paid AUD$1.3 million for the work, but the public and other artists were horrified at the price; 30 years later it is considered a great investment, valued at over AUD$60 million. 'It is a diary of Jackson's life, a masterpiece,' says Gleeson.

James Gleeson continued to serve on numerous boards until 1982; after years of only being a part-time painter he finally picked up the brush and began to paint full-time again. For over 20 years James has been delivering masterpieces. 'I start with a charcoal drawing; you resolve the technical problem in the drawing then you paint it, then you worry about the colour problem. People then bring their own imagination to the paintings; there is an interaction between what I add to the painting and what the viewer gets out of it.'

James Gleeson continues to paint almost every day and continues to display his work in national and private galleries throughout Australia. 'An artist's work must show a talent that reveals something of the nature of the creator; if it doesn't have the ability to do that then I don't think it is a work of art. It's pretentious to say it is.'

I have met James Gleeson at his Sydney home numerous times over the last five years and he has always been a gentleman. James is completely unpretentious and suave. He always inpsires me to create something surreal of my own, but I shan't. I'll leave it up to the master, James Gleeson.

Sir John Gorton

JOHN GREY GORTON was born on 9 September 1911 in Melbourne, Victoria. He attended Geelong Grammar School then moved to the United Kingdom; he finished his education at Oxford University. On his return to Australia Gorton helped with his father's orchard at Kerang. On 8 November 1940, Gorton enlisted in the RAAF; he served in World War II as a fighter pilot. During a mission his plane was shot down and crashed. He was lucky to survive, but was severely injured. His face was shattered and he had to have reconstructive surgery. He was discharged from the air force on 5 December 1944, with the rank of flight lieutenant.

On his return from war, John Gorton entered local government, where he was a member of Kerang Shire council from 1946 to 1952, becoming president in 1949. He joined the Liberal Party and in 1949 was narrowly defeated is his attempt to be elected to the Victorian Legislative Council. In December 1949 Gorton successfully stood as Senate candidate at the general election; he kept his seat, winning the next four Senate elections. During most of the 1960s, John served as a minister in the Liberal Party—Minister for the Navy, Minister for Interior, Minister for Works, Minister in charge of Commonwealth Activities in Education and Research and Minister for Education and Science. When the opportunity arose for John to become prime minister he jumped at the chance.

On 19 December 1967, a crisis was brewing in the Liberal Country Party. When caretaker Prime Minister John McEwen threatened the Liberals that the County Party would leave the coalition if Treasurer William McMahon was voted Liberal leader. Gorton and Paul Hasluck challenged for the position.

On 10 January 1968, John Gorton was sworn in as Australia's nineteenth prime minister. Gorton thus became the only senator ever to become prime minister. On 31 January he resigned from the Senate and moved to the House of Representatives; he held the seat of Higgins for three general elections until 1974.

John Gorton quickly became known as the people's prime minister; he enjoyed a drink with the public and was admired because of his bravery in World War II. But as time went on Gorton's leadership came under fire; the Vietnam War was intensifying and too many Australians were losing their lives in a war that most opposed. On 8 May 1970, Vietnam Moratorium Day, marches were held in all state capitals.

John did not see eye to eye with some state premiers in particular NSW, Victoria and Queensland. They clashed over his 'centralising' ambitions; the premiers were not happy with the Federal Government's legislation on offshore mineral rights and by May 1970 this issue was dividing his government. John was losing the confidence of his own government and that of the Australian people.

On 10 March 1971 his party voted on a motion of confidence in his leadership; they were tied at 33:33. Gorton put the party before himself and stood down from his position as prime minister. John Gorton was a war hero and our prime minister, but he wanted to be remembered as a man of the people.

Sir John Gorton died on 19 May 2002, aged 90.

I contacted Sir John Gorton in 1998 when I found his number in the telephone book. I rang him to request a photo shoot and to find out for myself if the number was John Gorton's, our ex-prime minister; to my astonishment it was. On my arrival he opened the door and two of his three dogs ran out the front door. 'Oh dear!' said Gorton. He excused himself and gave chase. I was left standing at the front door with the third dog growling at me. After ten minutes or so I heard Gorton and his two dogs coming back. 'Sorry about that,' said Gorton in a tired and worn-out voice. 'They always run out like that. How can I help you?' I reminded him of our meeting and phone call, which he didn't remember. Then again, he was eighty-seven and had just spent ten minutes chasing two dogs! Nevertheless he was happy to spend time with me, posing for photos and giving me a tour of his house. Truly a man of the people.

Germaine Greer
Author/feminist

THEY SAY that every man is intimidated by an intelligent woman, but surely, with all the women that I have met, I would not fall into that category. After all, I have met Faith Bandler, Margaret Olley and Nancy Wake but every so often you meet someone who enjoys challenging you on an intellectual level. Welcome to the world of Germaine Greer. She has been challenging men—and all of the so-called authorities—throughout her life. She has fought for every woman who has had enough of being treated merely as an object. In most cases Greer has won the battle; she is still fighting the war.

Germaine Greer was born on 29 January 1939 in Melbourne. Germaine did not live in a happy home and ran away twice. She was constantly searching for contentment, which she felt escaped her at home. Germaine did not have art, music or literature in her home life, and she believed she could find the joy she so longed for by studying these branches of knowledge. Germaine gained her education at the Star of the Sea Convent in Gardenvale. However, she was dismissed from class because she argued with a nun, who told Greer that communism was the devil's work.

After completing school, Germaine enrolled at Melbourne University in 1956. She graduated in 1958 with a bachelor of arts. She then moved to Sydney and graduated from Sydney University in 1963 with first-class honours. She then received a Commonwealth Scholarship to study at Cambridge University in England, where she received a PhD in 1968. Now armed with an education as well as a highly intelligent mind, Germaine was ready to rebel.

By the late 1960s the world was changing, due largely to the war in Vietnam. Millions of people around the world were searching for a change and hippies were fighting for peace and love. Germaine knew that women needed a change as well. In 1970 she released the bible of feminism, *The Female Eunuch*', in which she told women they didn't need men to control their lives. The only thing women needed was freedom to be themselves, and Germaine gave them their wings to be free.

Germaine became the spokesperson for women's liberation. Soon women were staging protests all around the world, burning their bras and telling their husbands to cook their own dinners. Germaine appeared on the cover of *Life* magazine on 7 May 1971 with the headline: 'Saucy feminist that even men like'. She was not trying to create a new race; she was trying to liberate women. Germaine was an international celebrity, appearing on television shows, and writing articles in magazines and papers. She helped many women open their eyes and respond to their inner thoughts with courage and vivacity. Germaine has always considered herself an anarchist; after the release of her sequel to *The Female Eunuch*, *The Whole Woman* she said: 'I am an anarchist basically. I don't think the future lies in constraining people in doing stuff they are not good at and don't want to do.'

Germaine continues to be outspoken on numerous issues, more recently the treatment and understanding of Indigenous Australians. She continues to present speeches on countless topics all around the world and is also a highly respected lecturer at the University of Warwick in England, where she has lived for most of her life.

In 2003, I contacted Germaine's agent and requested a photo shoot. I was to meet her at Randwick Racecourse. I arrived early to listen to her speech, but was surprised to see that the crowd consisted mostly of Sydney's socialites, as opposed to Sydney's university students, whose campus was just across the road. Had the Greer world come full circle? We completed the photo shoot and Greer walked back into the room to be idolised by all.

Reg Grundy

Television executive/entrepreneur

MOST AUSTRALIANS know his name, but very few of us know what he looks like, and that's exactly how Reg Grundy likes it.

Born Reginald Grundy in Sydney on 4 August 1923, Grundy was raised in Adelaide and attended St Peters School. After completing school, Grundy enlisted in the Citizen Military Forces in December 1941. He was discharged in August 1946 as a sergeant during demobilisation. After a while he got a job at David Jones, where he sharpened his selling skills.

In 1947 Grundy took a job broadcasting livestock events at the Sydney Royal Easter Show. This led to him signing a sponsorship deal to broadcast rugby league on the radio—a new concept. The only problem was that the radio station didn't have anyone to call the game. Reg volunteered and until a couple of hours before the kick-off, Grundy was still learning the rules, phrases and the players' names. Grundy stayed in radio and became the first radio broadcaster in Australia to call a world title fight in 1952.

By the mid-1950s, a new invention called television was taking over people's living rooms. While working in radio Reg had created numerous game shows, and he saw television as the next step for his career. He went to Channel Nine's chief executive, Ken G. Hall, with a show titled *Wheel of Fortune*. Hall liked the idea and Grundy found himself hosting the show six nights a week. But Reg knew the uncertainty of show business, and knew he needed more than one show running at once.

The Australian market was too small for Grundy's ideas to survive and he had to expand. He broke into the American market, but it was a long, hard road. As he puts it: 'I kept throwing punches until I hit.' Reg was creating more game shows and expanding his empire. In 1960 he founded Reg Grundy Enterprises; he soon became the leading producer for game shows in Australia, but things took a turn for the worse when all his shows were cancelled during the 1960s. This made him even more determined to succeed. Reg basically had to start over again, knocking on doors and selling his concepts.

Being the man that he is, he continued to pay all of his employees during these tough times. By the 1970s, Reg's company was once again beginning to make a profit. He expanded his production company and started to make daytime television soapies, including *The Young Doctors*, *The Restless Years* and *Prisoner*. In 1979 he opened his first overseas office in Los Angeles; it was his chance to go global. Grundy pioneered the term 'parochial internationalism'; this meant that through the international network that Grundy owned and operated, programs were made in each country, for that country, by its citizens. Reg would hire an Australian executive who spoke that language to understand what the people wanted in each country.

During the late 1970s Grundy started purchasing game shows and making them his own. His first was *Sale of the Century*. Reg continued to create new television shows, from game shows to dramas, and he was also buying other productions operating all over the world. With no children to continue his legacy, in 1995 he sold Grundy Worldwide to Pearson International for US$386 million. Reg still owns a number of radio networks across Australia, and is a highly skilled wildlife photographer.

In Monte Carlo in 2003, Reg Grundy was honoured with an award by Prince Albert, who said: 'What he created is now being attempted to be replicated by many companies around the world, it is only fitting that given the theme of our conference, "Formats Forum", we should honour the great contributions he made in this field of entertainment.' Reg Grundy has produced 120 television shows globally, including dramas, game shows, movies and documentaries.

When I think of Reg Grundy I smile. The whole time I was with him, his wife Joy Chambers and assistant Grahame, we spent laughing. Reg is one of the most humble and kind people I have ever met. They say that good guys come last, but nobody told Reg Grundy, because he is an honest and decent man, and a winner.

David Gulpilil

Actor

DAVID GULPILIL has amazing screen presence; he does not have to speak to capture the attention of the audience. Gulpilil has the charisma of old-fashioned movie stars of the early twentieth century and brings that magic into today's cinemas.

David Gulpilil was born on 1 July 1953 and was fortunate to have a traditional Aboriginal upbringing. He spent his childhood in the bush, learning to track, hunt and dance, becoming highly skilled in all. David also attended school at the Mission School at Maningrida in north east Arnhem Land. He was a highly intelligent young boy, who could already speak six indigenous languages by the time he was 15. From a very early age David's light shone brighter than most. He had a unique magnetism.

When British filmmaker Nicolas Roeg wanted to cast an unknown Aboriginal boy for his movie *Walkabout*, he searched long and far, eventually ending up Maningrida. When he saw Gulpilil dance and perform, he knew he had discovered his new star. The movie was first screened in 1970. It received rave reviews, as did David; *Walkabout* made him a celebrity. Already a highly talented dancer and performer, David was now in demand by the world's moviemakers. He followed his outstanding performance in *Walkabout* with the movie *Mad Dog Morgan* in 1976, which gave a further boost to his career.

The following year he featured in the hit movie *Storm Boy'*, adapted from the celebrated book. *Storm Boy* was a huge success. David was now an even bigger screen idol and he was being invited to parties and premieres, mixing with other famous actors, both here and around the world.

However, living the life of a famous actor was not what Gulpilil wanted; he felt more at ease with his family and friends on the land. He was now living two separate lives, one of a movie star and the other as an Indigenous Australian, trying to survive off the land. David continued to act; he was in great demand and featured in such movies as *Crocodile Dundee* (1986), *Dead Heart* (1996), *Rabbitproof Fence* (2002) and *The Tracker* (2002). *The Tracker* was the first starring role for David since *Walkabout* some 30 years earlier. David has also appeared in numerous television shows and has written two volumes of children's stories based on Yolngu beliefs (his culture).

In between acting jobs, David has travelled throughout Australia, performing at festivals. For David, fame has found him, but not fortune; he feels he has been taken advantage of by many people in the entertainment industry. He does not live the life of a movie star. He lives in a man-made shack in Ramingining in Arnhem Land.

Hunter, tracker, ceremonial dancer, musician, writer, story teller, actor: David Gulpilil is all of these. David is a mentor to young Aboriginals and is a respected tribal leader in his home in the Northern Territory. Like most of us he has had his ups and downs, but there is no doubting that David Gulpilil is an inspiration to us all. A further testament to this is Craig Ruddy's controversial charcoal portrait of him which was the winner of the 2004 Archibald prize.

I met David Gulpilil in 2004 at the Belvoir Street Theatre, where he was performing his autobiographical stage production. I met him after one of his sell-out shows and photographed him in the theatre. The photoshoot was full of fun and laughter and we enjoyed our time together. David was very lively and excited and had many admirers to talk to.

Brian Henderson

IF YOU believe that 'everything happens for a reason' you'll understand the Brian Henderson story, because sometimes it actually does!

Brian Henderson was born on 14 September 1931, in New Zealand. When he was a young boy he contracted tuberculosis while attending boarding school, Waitaki Boys High. During his three-year illness, 'Hendo', as he likes to be called, entertained the other patients by spinning discs over a makeshift radio station. At the tender age of 16, Hendo joined Dunedin's 4ZB radio station; he was the youngest radio announcer in New Zealand.

Hendo arrived in Sydney in the early 1950s and in 1953 he got a job working the breakfast and night-time shift at 2CH. In January 1957, shortly after television was launched in Australia, Hendo was hired by Channel Nine; this was to be his big break. Hendo started off by reading the weekend news bulletin.

In November 1958 Hendo began to present and produce the show *Accent on Youth*, which quickly became known as *Bandstand*. *Bandstand* was ahead of its time; it was a music show that featured local and international music acts performing the hits of the day; you might call it the MTV of the 1960s. *Bandstand* was an hour-long show and was telecast on 28 stations across Australia. It launched many careers, the most famous being the Bee Gees. Hendo hosted and produced the show for 14 years and by doing so became a household name. Through *Bandstand*, Hendo won the 1967 Gold Logie award.

In 1964 Channel Nine's prime time newsreader, Chuck Faulkner, left the network and Hendo was chosen as his replacement. From 1964 until 29 November 2002, Hendo was welcomed into Sydneysiders' living rooms. For five nights a week Hendo would tell viewers what was going on in Australia and around the world. Sydneysiders felt that they could trust what Hendo had to say; in an uncertain world he was dependable. Hendo helped make Channel Nine's news the most successful news program in Australian history, and he is the longest serving newsreader in Australian television history. The network slogan confirmed what viewers thought: 'Brian told me so.'

For all of the news events that occured from 1964 until the end of 2002, Hendo was there to cover it. He was always calm and it was clear that he had a sense of humour; the ironic thing is that even though viewers felt they knew him—almost as if he were a part of the family—no one really did. Hendo is a very private man. He wanted to read the news, not be a part of it.

When Hendo retired in November 2002, his boss, Kerry Packer, who is also a very private man, released a statement: 'I know that we all hoped that Hendo would go on forever. After all, he's only been with us for forty-six years, so why couldn't he score his half century?' Hendo left our living rooms at the age of 71. All good things must come to an end, and as Hendo puts it, 'that's the way it is.'

I met Hendo in 2000 at Channel Nine's Sydney studio. My friend Grayem Linton, who commissions portraits painted on car boot lids, had arranged to meet Hendo so he could get him to sign his boot lid. Hendo graciously signed the boot lid. I took a shot or two and asked Hendo if I could put a photo in this project. He was flattered by the invitation and told me if I needed anything else to just ask. He was very welcoming and caring and I truly appreciated his genuineness. I chose not to do another photoshoot. I thought this photo was unique, plus I didn't want to intrude on his spare time. After all he had given us 46 years!

Nora Heysen

Artist

THE ART WORLD is ruled by men; if asked to name a famous artist, most people would not name a woman. For a young girl from Adelaide to become the first female to win the Archibald Prize, in 1938, was a massive achievement. (It was a further 22 years before another female won.) But winning the award was the easy part; Nora Heysen spent much of her life living in the shadow of her famous father, celebrated landscapist Sir Hans Heysen: 'I was known as the talented daughter of the famous Hans Heysen.'

Nora Heysen was on born 11 January 1911 in Adelaide and was the fourth of eight children.

She had a fascinating childhood, growing up surrounded by celebrities. It was not unusual to find Sir Lawrence Olivier, Vivien Leigh or Dame Nellie Melba at the family home. In fact, Dame Nellie Melba gave Nora her first pallet, which she still had when I met her. 'Nellie Melba was the first famous person that I remember coming to the house. The first thing that I noticed about Melba was that she had a ladder in her stocking—that humanised her,' recalled Nora. 'She was intrigued by my work and bought one of my paintings.'

Nora started painting when she was about 14. Sadly for Nora her famous father was never very generous in his praise. Nora recalls: 'He said my paintings were alright, but that's about as far as he got. My father was hoping one of his sons would become the artist. He said that it was too difficult for women.' But it wasn't just her father who thought like this. 'They [male artists] didn't want women in the art world; they did their best to keep us out.'

Nora started painting gum trees just like her father. 'Then I wanted to get away from his work and make my own.' She did just that, creating a style of her own. 'I used to enjoy painting eggs. I used to wait until I heard the hens cackle, so I'd get the bloom on the freshly laid eggs. But my favourite subjects to paint are flowers—you can be alone with flowers,' recalled Nora with a smile.

Nora's first exhibition was a success; she took her earnings and studied at the Central School for Arts in London, for two years. On her return she painted a portrait that changed the history books, and her life, forever. In 1938 Nora painted the Ambassador of The Netherland's wife, Madame Elink Schuurman. She entered it in the Archibald Prize and won it. Being the first person to do anything is always difficult, but to beat the men at their own game was a huge achievement. Her win drew a massive amount of criticism, mainly from her jealous male counterparts. Fellow artist Max Meldrum told the press: 'if I were a woman I would certainly prefer raising a family to a career in art. To expect women to do some things as well as men is sheer lunacy!'

Nora received criticism for winning the Archibald rather than the praise and adoration that she rightly deserved. Even her own father was not forthcoming in his praise for his young talented daughter. 'I couldn't believe it when I won. I think my father was pleased, but he didn't make any comments.'

In October 1943 Nora became the first female official war artist. She painted in places such as New Guinea, Lae and Borneo until 1946; and some critics believe that she created some of her best work during this time. 'I would always have my sketchbook with me wherever I went'.

''It took me a long while to get out of my father's shadow. I had to defeat a lot of men. It's not as hard for women artists today, but they're still not on equal par with male artists.' She feels she has been an inspiration to female artists: 'If I can do it, perhaps they can.'

The first time I met Nora Heysen was a great thrill for me. I had heard that she was a recluse and had been very selective in her choice of photographers and interviewers over the years. However, I was able to contact her and convinced her to see me. When I asked Nora what she wanted to be remembered for, she simply answered, 'That I tried.' Nora inspired not only female artists, but all artists, to achieve their dreams. Nora Heysen died in December 2003, aged 92.

Barry Humphries
Entertainer/author

An ACTOR becomes famous for playing another character; Barry Humphries has become infamous for playing another gender. Perhaps that's why he has stayed in the public eye for so long—there is still a fascination with seeing a man dressed as a woman. In Shakespeare's time male actors would play the parts of females, so the attraction has been there for hundreds of years.

Barry has developed several characters. In 1956 he created his most successful character so far: Mrs Edna Everage, a Melbourne housewife, who would become a dame in 1976! Her greeting to fans—'Hello possums!'—is now a part of the Australian vernacular. Humphries' other exceptionally successful character is the disgusting fiend Sir Les Patterson, who was created almost two decades later, in 1974. Other mocking characters include Aussie comic strip star Barry McKenzie, narrow-minded unionist Lance Boyle, and the ever serene and loving Sandy Stone.

Barry achieved infamy when he unveiled Edna Everage to British audiences at the Fortune Theatre in 1969 for his one-man show *Just a Show*. British critics just didn't quite 'get it', though it did lead to a fleeting BBC TV series *The Barry Humphries Scandals*.

Over the next couple of decades Edna Everedge made several television appearances in Australia and the United Kingdom, plus two extremely successful series of the talk show *The Dame Edna Experience* for London TV, with a host of celebrity guests including Liza Minnelli, Robin Williams and Cher. Dame Edna has also appeared in television series such as *Ally McBeal*, *Roseanne*, *The Tonight Show* and *Hollywood Squares*, and was recently the voice of Bruce, the Great White Shark, in *Finding Nemo*.

In 2000 Edna received the Special Tony Award for a live theatre event for her Broadway debut in *Dame Edna: The Royal Tour*. Her latest Broadway production, *Dame Edna: Back with a Vengeance,* was sold out and critically acclaimed; some critics compared Humphries to comic genius Charlie Chaplin. Dame Edna has been welcomed with open arms in New York; she was even invited to light the Christmas tree in Times Square. Not bad for a Melbourne housewife!

Barry creates his characters to 'encourage people to look at Australia critically and with affection and humour, which is what all comedians should do'. Born in suburban Melbourne on 17 February 1934, Barry John Humphries was educated at the University of Melbourne where he studied law, philosophy and fine arts. Robert Hughes (art critic/historian) notes in his study of Australian art that Humphries 'seemed to understand the ferocity of the original Dadaists.'

Barry says, 'I think he was right. I certainly shocked a few people in Melbourne and have gone on shocking people ever since in another branch of creative endeavour.'

Barry is multitalented; he is a painter, an actor and the author of numerous plays, autobiographies and novels. His autobiography, *More Please*, written in 1992, won the JR Ackerley prize for biography in 1993. In 1982 Humphries was given the Order of Australia and was given an Honorary Doctorate by Griffith University (Australia) in 1994. He is married to Lizzie Spender, the daughter of British poet Sir Stephen Spender, and they have four children.

Barry has been a part of Australia's cultural landscape for close to 50 years, for his satirical characters, his much-loved landscape paintings, and his writing. He has inspired and captivated people from all walks of life worldwide.

I photographed Barry in the late 1990s after one of his Dame Edna shows at Sydney's State Theatre, I told him what the photo was going to be used for and he asked me 'How do I look?' 'Different,' I replied. 'Well then you'd better get your shot,' Humphries replied with a cheeky grin. I have met Humphries on several occasions over the last ten years and have found that like his characters he is always changing. 'Who is Barry Humphries?' Well, no-one really knows, and that's what makes him so intriguing to millions of people around the world.

Bob Jane
Racing driver/tyre magnate

BOB JANE is a racing driver, patron, promoter, team owner, car dealer, tyre dealer and entrepreneur. Born Robert Frederick Jane on 18 December 1929 in Melbourne, Bob Jane, to most of us, is the place we go to purchase tyres. But it was motor racing that propelled Bob Jane the man onto the world's stage. During the 1950s Jane started racing in amateur and professional bicycle races—he was quite successful and held numerous state records. Along with racing, Jane had a keen interest in business; he was taught by his uncle to work with leather, making such things as handbags, gloves, shoes, footballs and seat covers. And it was the seat covers that gave Bob the most profit. He started a company called American Luxury Seat Covers in Brunswick. Bob had his first taste of the business world.

Bob started racing cars in 1956, with a Maserati 300S. Then in 1961 he built the most famous 3.8 racing Jaguar in the world. In it he won over 300 races in Australia, including the 1962 and 1967 Australian Championships. Also in 1961 Bob was racing in the Armstrong 500 in a Mercedes Benz 220SE. On the second lap Bob got a flat tyre, so he went into the pits, got out of his car and spent five minutes changing the tyre himself. He then got back in the race and was behind the other cars by several laps. The race seemed to be lost, but Bob did not give up—he and co-driver Harry Firth eventually won the Armstrong 500.

In 1962, Bob again won the Armstrong 500, this time in a Falcon XP. That same year Bob became the Victorian distributor for the Italian Pirelli, German Fulda, Dutch Vrederstein and French Kleeber Tyres. Bob realised the potential in Australia for a company that could provide tyres of a high standard at a good price. The following year (1963) he won the first Bathurst race in a Cortina GT. In 1964 he would win his second Bathurst. Bob Jane has won many other races, and is the only driver to win the Australian Touring Car Championship four times in succession: twice at Phillip Island and twice at Bathurst. During his time as a racing car driver Bob Jane was second to none; he had 41 wins from 41 starts, a record that has never been broken. Bob continued racing and in 1985

came second outright in the Hardie 1000. He retired from motor racing in 1988 at age 57.

The year 1965 saw Bob Jane open his first tyre outlet in Melbourne. Others followed in Brisbane and Sydney. Today the Bob Jane T-Mart Company operates not only in Australia, but also in New Zealand and the west coast of the United States. There are over one hundred Bob Jane T-Marts—it is Australia's most successful franchise for motor tyres.

In 1969, Bob opened and operated Southern Motors; a public company and a General Motors dealership. During the 1970s Southern Motors was the world's largest General Motors dealership. He successfully ran this dealership until 1981.

Bob is now the owner and operator of both the Calendar Park Raceway (Thunderdome) in Victoria and the Adelaide International Raceway in South Australia. He is also the leading figure in NASCAR Racing in Australia; until recently Bob Jane's NASCAR circuit was the only one like it outside America. Taking over four years to construct and two years to plan, with an investment of approximately $54 million, it opened in 1987.

I met Bob Jane at his Melbourne office in 2000. When I arrived I noticed some tyres sitting in the lobby. When we entered Bob's boardroom he asked me where he should stand. I looked around and then remembered the tyres. I ran out and carried a tyre into the boardroom. I placed it on the table and asked Bob to pose with it. Bob told me that nobody had ever done a photo of him like that before and he thought it was a clever idea. It was a great compliment from a man who knew a great idea when he saw one.

Thomas Keneally

Author

THOMAS KENEALLY was born in Sydney on 7 October 1935. His schooling was at St Patrick's at Strathfield and it was during his time at school that Tom started writing, mainly influenced by adventure books such as *Treasure Island*. After completing school, Tom entered the seminary in 1952; while he was there he started a literary club and found that he had a passion for writing. After leaving the seminary in 1959, Tom became a school teacher at Waverley College. Throughout his time as a teacher Keneally was writing short stories—he had a couple published in *The Bulletin*. This gave him the confidence to write his first novel. 'I wrote my first novel during the school holidays of 1962-63. I sent my novel overseas, and by mid-winter the publishers accepted it.' Tom's first book was called *The Place at Whitton*, and was published in Australia and the United States in 1964. The book introduced Thomas Keneally as an author. 'When the book was published I thought, well, this is what you do, so I pursued it.'

In 1965, Tom married Judy, and in the same year released *The Fear*. He followed that success with *Bring Larks and Heroes*. 'From then on, gradually, over a short period, I became a full-time writer, but I did everything to survive; as any writer will tell you. I did reviews, screenplays and plays—I did whatever it took to keep the bread on the table.' From the very beginning, Tom believed that writing was like running his own business, and he always tried to expand his potential market, by getting his books distributed overseas. 'I've never found in my writing a conflict between writing about the world and writing about Australia. For me it was never a choice— it was mostly Australia in the world and sometimes the world in Australia. When I was young, there was an idea that you either wrote for Australia or you wrote to sell elsewhere, but sometimes you wrote books like *Schindler's Ark*. At the time it was written, it was considered that Australians didn't write those sorts of books.'

Tom continued to write international bestselling books, including *The Chant of Jimmie Blacksmith* (1972), which was later made into a movie by Fred Schepisi in 1978 and was shortlisted for the 1972 Booker Prize. Tom was shortlisted for the Booker Prize in 1975 with *Gossip from the Forest* and again in 1979 with *Confederates*. He eventually won the Booker Prize in 1982 with *Schindler's Ark*. 'I had done a little book tour of the US and bought a briefcase from a man who was a Holocaust survivor. His name was Leopold Pfefferberg; he was a Schindler survivor and told me about Oskar Schindler. Over the next two years Pfefferberg assisted me while I wrote the book. In 1983 the film rights for *Schindler's Ark* were bought and in 1992 Spielberg rang me up and said, 'I'm going to make the film'. In 1993, *Schindler's List* (the movie) was released. It was an international success, winning seven Academy Awards, including best movie and best director for Spielberg. Spielberg is quoted as saying that he could not have made the movie without Keneally and Pfefferberg. *Schindler's Ark* has sold well over four million copies and the book has sold more copies than any other Booker Prize-winning novel.

Thomas Keneally is still writing books today. 'I've written too many books for the public to keep up, but I like writing many books, I would be uneasy if I didn't write many books; at least a book a year. But not all of them are going to be made into famous movies by Steven Spielberg,' he adds with a laugh. Thomas Keneally is one of the most successful authors in Australia and one of the most respected worldwide. He has won numerous other awards including the Miles Franklin Award twice and the *LA Times* Fiction Prize. Besides writing over 25 fiction books, Tom has also written 13 non-fiction books, a screenplay, children's books, and has even written two books under the pseudonym William Coyle.

I met Tom in 2000 at an awards ceremony for the Olympics and told him of my project; he happily agreed to pose for me and gave me his phone number. I was finally able to photograph him in 2004. I found him to be very down-to-earth and a natural storyteller.

Edward Kenna

War hero

EDWARD KENNA was born on 6 July 1919 in Hamilton, Victoria. Ted (as he is known) attended St Mary's Convent School. After completing school, Ted started working as a plumber. He also used to enjoy shooting rabbits with his friends, 'I became pretty good with a rifle,' he remembers.

On 9 August 1940 Ted and his brother Jack enlisted in the 2nd Australian Imperial Force. On 3 September 1943 Ted and Jack were posted to the 2/4th unit. The unit was sent to Cairo, where they trained for jungle warfare. On 30 October 1943, they were sent to Papua New Guinea. Ted was posted to A Company, which was ordered to move to Driniumor River, where they were to carry out security patrol tasks east and west of the river.

By 12 November, the A Company had moved further east and come into conflict with the Japanese; by 15 December they'd successfully defeated the Japanese. Only 11 Australians had been killed, in contrast to the 98 Japanese who had died. Ted, still with the A Company, continued to fight in some horrific battles. On 10 May 1944 the battalion launched a successful attack on Wewak Point; a steep area full of bunkers and caves. The A Company's next mission was to capture the Wirui mission. On 14 May 1945 A, B and C Companies joined forces. That day was hot and humid, and visibility was limited by the long grass that covered the fields. Ted's platoon was ordered to move forward to try to capture enemy machine gun posts. As they surged ahead, they came very close to the enemy and were continually attacked by heavy machine-gun fire. The A Company suffered heavy losses and could neither advance nor retreat. Ted tried to return fire with his Bren gun, but was prevented by the high grass.

Without order or hesitation Ted stood up in full view of the enemy and began to shoot his Bren gun from his hip. After all of the bullets had been fired, Ted, still in full view, grabbed a rifle and continued firing. Luckily, Ted was not injured but bullets passed between his arm and body. This did not faze him and he continued to attack. Incredibly, Ted single-handedly captured the bunker without any further losses to the A Company.

On 5 June the A Company attacked the Japanese near Mt Kwakubo. 'We got the order to attack. There was a big tree in the field and I got behind the tree with three other men, thinking we were out of the enemy's view. I saw something out of the corner of my eye.' Kenna had been shot in the face: 'The bullet entered through my jaw, hit my teeth, deflected back and blew out the right-hand side of my mouth. Because of the deflection it went back into my right shoulder, tearing the flesh and blew out of my chest. My mate said, "You've been hit!" and the next thing I knew, he was shot and killed. I crawled back to base with my face blown off and found a doctor; then the Fuzzy Wuzzies carried me back to camp.'

It took two weeks for Ted to get back to Brisbane Hospital. He spent a year and a half there, having countless operations, grafting bone from his hip to his jaw. While in hospital, Ted met Nurse Marjorie—they married on 2 June 1947. On 6 January, 1947 the Governor General and the Duke of Gloucester presented Edward Kenna with the Victoria Cross. His citation reads: 'for his magnificent courage and complete disregard for his own safety'.

In 2000, Australia Post released a set of stamps to commemorate Australia's Victoria Cross winners; only four winners were chosen for the stamps and Edward Kenna was one of them.

I met Ted and Marjorie at their home in Victoria in 2000. Ted was a respectful and gentle person, who never once boasted about his heroic actions during the war. That's what makes a true hero; someone who just does what they think they have to do. Not someone who does something to expect acclaim.

Phillip Law

Antarctic explorer

BORN PHILLIP Garth Law in Victoria in 1912, Phillip went to Hamilton High School. As a child he and his brother Geoff used to go mountaineering and bushwalking in the nearby area of Hamilton. Phillip was fascinated by the mountains and began skiing in the Australian Alps. After school, he went to Melbourne University and became the lightweight boxing champion. After completing a science degree, Phillip became a secondary school teacher. From 1929 to 1938 he taught at Melbourne Boys High School.

From 1939 to 1947 Phillip worked in research at Melbourne University under Professor Laby.

As a young man, he and fellow teacher Bruce Osborne decided they wanted to be the first people to climb Mt Kosciusko on skis. In 1938 they set out in the middle of winter and fought through trees and snow, eventually ending up at Mt Townsend, only to find themselves caught in a blizzard. The two men found shelter behind rocks, took off their wet clothes and changed into warmer clothes. Defeated, they climbed back down the mountain, through a river and back to their huts: 'It was a foolish thing to do, but I learnt a valuable lesson, which was never go climbing in those conditions with only two people.'

In 1947 a group of Australians were planning an expedition to Antarctica. Phillip had read every book he could get his hands on about Antarctica, and had heard rumours about the expedition. He knew he had to get involved, but didn't know how to go about it. Phillip was intending to write a letter to famed Australian explorer Sir Douglas Mawson, but didn't need to; a professor at Melbourne University told Phillip to go to Canberra as they needed a chief scientist to head the Antarctic expedition. Five weeks later, Phillip was the chief scientist for the 1947 Antarctic exploration team.

'When I got my first job, as a chief scientist in the Antarctic Division, my friends all called me foolish for leaving my job at Melbourne University to take on a job like this, but I somehow knew that this Antarctic thing was going to develop into something very important and I wanted to be a part of it.'

In 1948 the Group Captain, Stuart Campbell, who was in charge of the expedition, left his position and Phillip took over as leader. He ran it until 1966. Antarctica is the most barren and isolated place in the world. So in 1948 when Phillip and the other scientists arrived in Antarctica, they had to invent new techniques to travel above the water and in the sun. 'We were the first people to design huts which gave individuals private cubicles. Before that everything in Antarctica was on a bunkhouse design. We were the first to build an aircraft hangar and it is still there.' Phillip led expeditions to Antarctica from 1947 to 1966 and was the director of the Australian National Antarctic Research Expeditions (ANARE). He, along with his team, mapped more than 3000 miles of coastline and approximately 800 000 square miles of territory.

Phillip was the founder of Davis Station, which is Australia's largest Antarctic base. He was also involved in the first scuba dive in Antarctic waters and the first Australia to Antarctica flight. His wife Nel was the first Australian woman to visit Antarctica. 'I am fortunate to say that I was the first person to ever see some parts of Antarctica. Can you imagine? My eyes were the very first human eyes to ever see certain parts of Antarctica!' Law is a scientist, explorer, adventurer, teacher and author.

In 2002 when I met and photographed Phillip in Melbourne, he was 90 years old. We went outside so he could show us his new sports car; he told me that just recently, he had been clocked at 150 in a 110 km/h zone! Law still loves an adventure and is enthusiastic about Antarctica and regularly makes trips back. 'The same curiosity that makes a scientist is the curiosity that makes an explorer,' he says. Law has been a lucky man and I found him to have a razor-sharp and active memory. He is still 100 per cent enthusiastic about Antarctica and loves to share his adventures with others.

Ray Lawler

Playwright

RAYMOND EVENOR LAWLOR was born 23 May 1921 in the Melbourne suburb of Footscray. He grew up in the district and was educated at Geelong Road State School, an education that finished at the age of 13, when he went to work in a local factory during the Great Depression. Ray worked as a factory labourer there for the next eleven years. During this time he discovered a growing interest in theatre, began training as an actor, and started to write plays. His amateur pursuits were a night-time activity; labouring was his chief means of support. Several of his plays were presented by Melbourne amateur companies, but Australian professional theatre at that time was devoted to the presentation of overseas hit plays, and offered little encouragement for local playwrights.

Leaving his factory employment in the mid-1940s, Ray eventually secured his first professional theatre engagement: in a year of variety shows at the Cremorne Theatre in Brisbane, under the management of noted American comedian Will Mahoney. It was during this time that Ray met two cane-cutters who were courting chorus girls, an acquaintance that bore fruit several years later when he came to write *Summer of the Seventeenth Doll*.

After leaving variety, Ray returned to Melbourne and worked with the National Theatre Movement as both an actor and director. In 1949 he won an Australia-wide drama competition with a play called *The Cradle of Thunder*, which was presented at the Princess Theatre. This encouraged him to turn again to writing plays so he took a year off active theatre work in 1952-53 to write a first draft of *Summer of the Seventeenth Doll*. A second draft followed, after he had joined the recently formed Union Theatre Repertory Company, again working as both an actor and a director. This second draft of *Summer of the Seventeenth Doll* was submitted as an entry in the Australian Playwrights Advisory Board Competition of 1955, where it was awarded joint first prize with Oriel Gray's play *The Torrents*.

John Sumner, founder of the Union Theatre Repertory Company, pressed to have *The Doll*—as the play became known—presented by the Australian Elizabethan Theatre Trust in Melbourne, and Sumner directed its first production at the Union Theatre in late 1955, with Ray playing as the part of Barney Ibbot.

The success of the season led to this production being taken on an Australia-wide tour, and resulted in an offer by noted English actor and entrepreneur Laurence Olivier to sponsor the Australian presentation in the West End for a London season. This offer aroused much interest—it was the first time an Australian play with its local cast had gone overseas in this way, and national doubts and expectations were high. Fortunately, *The Doll* had a successful London opening and season at the New Theatre in 1957, and at the end of the year won the prestigious Evening Standard Award for the Best Play of 1957.

The Australian production then went immediately to America for a New York season, and failed on Broadway in 1958; mainly, Ray believes, because of American unfamiliarity with the Australian accent and slang. Ray then lived overseas for a number of years, mostly in England and Ireland, returning to Australia in 1975 at the invitation of John Sumner, to work with the Melbourne Theatre Company, and to write the two companion plays that now form *The Doll* Trilogy: *Kid Stakes* and *Other Times*.

I met Ray Lawler in his Melbourne home in 2000, and found him reluctant to accept that *The Doll* is now a classic. 'I suppose it must have been something, as it is being studied in schools and still being presented on stage some fifty years after it was written. I'm lucky, I suppose, to have found characters and a theme that are so enduringly and recognisably Australian. 'Lucky too for us that he did—Lawler's *Summer of the Seventeenth Doll* has become part of Australia's literary history.

John Laws

WHEN JOHN Laws starts his show in the morning, with 'Hello world', he is the voice of the Aussie battler, he is the voice of the land.

Born Richard John Sinclair Laws, in Wau, New Guinea on 8 August 1935, John spent the first five years of his life in New Guinea. In December 1941 Laws and his mother, Nessie, were evacuated from New Guinea because the Japanese had attacked. John ended up in Sydney, where he attended Knox Grammar.

When John was sixteen he went jackarooing. By the time he was 20 he'd hitchhiked through three states looking for work. He wanted a job in radio, but work in radio was hard to find. In Melbourne John was a fuel attendant, then he was a bus conductor in Brisbane, then he landed a job at 3BO radio station in Bendigo in 1953. John became restless at 3BO. He left after 18 months, then decided to travel around Australia. Laws' first break came in 1957, when he signed with 2UE. He then moved onto 2SM before ending up at 2KO in Newcastle.

In 1962 John moved back to Sydney, where he joined 2GB. After two years there, he left and joined 2UE. John was on a roll, but his luck was about to change. As a child John had suffered greatly from polio. Years later it returned and for a short time John was paralysed on one side. He was hospitalised, but kept very positive and very active. He wrote reviews, composed songs and even signed a four-year contract with Festival Records.

Once he recovered, he was back on the radio, recording songs and compering the television show *Star Time*, which earnt him a Gold Logie.

While at 2UE John developed his own style of talkback radio. He made listeners feel special when they phoned in and talked to him about topics of the day. It was a chance for everyday Australians to have their say. John switched stations numerous times: after leaving 2UE he ended up at 2UW, then 2UE, and 2GB, finally returning to 2UE. John brought something different to every station. He became the voice of the people and politicians used his radio shows to spread their word and new policies to the Australian public.

John is a unique figure. For nearly fifty years he has been at the top of his industry, keeping the public in touch. His shows are real; they are about real topics and real people. John Laws is Australia's most famous radio broadcaster. No other Australian radio broadcaster has won more radio awards than John Laws—he is the most celebrated and dominant radio commentator Australia has ever known, which has earnt him the affectionate nickname of 'Golden Tonsils'. His penchant for attracting the masses has also made him the world's highest paid radio broadcaster.

Radio broadcaster, columnist, author, poet, singer, television star, entertainer, salesman and the voice of the people—John Laws has done the lot. He has been at the top of the ratings for almost his entire working life. John is the Bradman of radio and it is unlikely that we will see his like again.

I wrote a letter to John in 2001, and a few days later he invited me to his apartment in Woolloomooloo. After clearing four security checkpoints, I was finally able to meet him. John was extremely kind and down-to-earth, allowing me plenty of time and even coming up with suggestions for the photo shoot. At one stage, John was going through my photos when he asked: 'Are you going to photograph RM Williams?' 'I hope so,' I replied. 'You have to,' he said. 'He is a real Australian Legend.' Ironically in 2002 when I did photograph RM he asked me 'have you photographed John Laws?' 'Yes' I happily replied. 'Good. The Australian people love him'.

George Lazenby

Actor

I T'S AMAZING to think that George Lazenby's first movie role was playing James Bond in the 1969 Bond movie *On Her Majesty's Secret Service*. He was also the youngest actor to portray Bond—at just thirty years old. George Lazenby was born on 5 September 1939. At age thirteen George watched his first Bond film; it was every kid's dream to become James Bond and he was no exception. From then on he modelled himself on James Bond. As a teenager Lazenby lived life to the full; riding motor cycles and dirt bikes, hang gliding, riding horses, playing football and performing stunts for his friends. he was searching for an adventurous life. After working with his father for a railway company for a while, George yearned for a bit more excitement. At 16 he joined the Australian Army and was placed in the Special Forces Unit. During his time in the army, George trained in martial arts and by the age of nineteen he had become a black belt and a martial arts instructor in the army.

George left the army and moved to Canberra, where he got a job as an auto mechanic, then was promoted to car salesman. This was not the adventure that George was yearning for, but he stuck it out, saving some money to try his luck in London. In 1964 George moved to London, where he began a career in modelling. Within two years George became the highest paid male model in Europe. In 1966 he was signed by the Fry's Chocolate Bar company to do television commercials for them; the commercials ran for three years on English television, making George a household name in Britain. While George was getting his hair cut he had a chance meeting with Bond series producer Cubby Broccoli.

In 1967 George was voted England's top male sex symbol; at last he was well on his way to living the James Bond lifestyle. That same year Sean Connery quit the role of Bond and producers searched all around the world for a new James Bond, but Broccoli had already found his replacement. The producers called George to audition for the role. With no acting experience, except for his television commercials, he won the part. George beat over 400 other actors for the chance to play James Bond.

George was so eager to prove himself as an actor that he broke the nose of a stuntman during auditions! George Lazenby was now 007; however, things did not run too smoothly while filming the movie. There was some tension on the set between Lazenby and director Peter Hunt, which made filming very uncomfortable.

On Her Majesty's Secret Service was released to mixed reviews in 1969. Sean Connery had played the role of 007 in the previous Bond movies, so it took a while for fans to warm to the movie, but eventually they did. George's film is regarded by James Bond fans as the best film in the entire series, due to its very authentic action scenes—performed mostly by George. He was on top of the world, and the Bond producers offered him a seven-movie deal, with United Artists offering him other films in between Bond movies.

But George took what turned out to be the wrong advice from his management, turning down all the offers. The hippie movement was growing and the number one movie during this time was *Easy Rider*. George and his management thought that the Bond movies were a thing of the past, and George stepped aside. Cubby Broccoli later remarked that George could have been the best Bond, had he not quit after just one film.

Although never again reaching the same heights of fame, George continues to act and still appears in television shows such as *Baywatch* (1999) and *The Pretender* (1999). In 2002 George married tennis champion Pam Shriver; they live in California.

In 2000, I was at a charity event and George was on the list. I approached him and told him of my project; he happily gave me his phone number and a day or two later I arrived at his friend's flat. We did the photo shoot and I asked him the obvious, 'Do you regret not going on with the James Bond movies?' 'Yes,' replied Lazenby, 'but at the time I thought that they were all over. That's okay; I've had a pretty good life.' George was very nice and charming but then he would be—after all he was Bond, James Bond.

Jimmy Little

Singer

JIMMY LITTLE was born on 1 March 1937 near the Murray River. His mother's tribe were river people and his father's were coastal people: 'I'm water, not fire, but inside I've got a ball of fire, which is passion. I'm a Pisces, and I was born on the river.' Jimmy recalls his childhood as being blessed. Both his parents were performers and young Jimmy used to watch his father on stage entertaining the crowds. 'I was born to entertain—my people were a music clan. Others got into sports and other activities, but for us it was music'.

Although he did go to school at missions and convents, Jimmy states: 'I graduated from the university of life at fifteen.' He caught a train to Sydney and started out in talent quests, which in those days were run by radio stations. If the stations liked your song, they would play it on their station, and then if a record company liked what they heard, they would record the song and release it to the public. Jimmy started his musical career as a country singer; he signed with EMI for two years, then in 1959 Festival Records offered him a deal he couldn't refuse. 'Festival said, "You can sing anything that you want"—I didn't just have to do country.' So Jimmy started recording the evergreen classics (the golden oldies); he sang songs that people wanted to hear. Jimmy released an album titled *Ballads with a Beat*; this album reached the top ten in the popular music charts and Jimmy started touring Australia, which he has continued to do for more than fifty years.

In 1959 Jimmy featured in the movie *Shadow of The Boomerang*. 'My character was a drover who worked on a cattle station. It was about living in a white world with a black view—he had one foot in two worlds.' In 1963 Festival Records approached Jimmy with a song that they believed was a good song for him to record; the song was called 'Royal Telephone'. The song was a huge hit, selling over 75 000 copies and making Jimmy Little an instant celebrity. That very same year, Jimmy was voted Australian pop star of the year.

'It was beyond everyone's imagination. It was the right time and I was in the right place. The song established me as a recording artist and people wanted to hear more gospel songs. Even the kids in Sunday school would learn it; for the kids it was like a jingle.'

'Royal Telephone' became Jimmy's signature tune and, perhaps remarkably for the time, Jimmy didn't face any racism. 'Around the time of 'Royal Telephone', television took off and I appeared on almost every television show.' Combined with his hit records, Jimmy became popular with the Australian public. 'They loved me because I was a good Christian boy and I was singing gospel songs. The public bought my records and supported me. People would see me on TV, in the magazines, then they would buy my records and come to see my shows.' Jimmy felt that he was a referee between white and black society. 'I felt like an unofficial politician. At first I was unique—a black singer in the mainstream. I was a novelty for a while, then after the novelty wore off, people discovered that I had talent.'

Jimmy Little has gone on to record over forty albums, from country to rock, pop to gospel. He's a diverse entertainer who has kept in touch with the Australian public for over 50 years. And in the last couple of years his career has surged again. Jimmy, who still records and tours, finds that his audience is now made up of people of all ages—from young children to grandparents. 'People still come up to me after the shows and say, wow, I finally got to meet the man who sang 'Royal Telephone'.

In 2004 Jimmy was named a National Living Treasure and awarded an Order of Australia. Jimmy has had a charmed life. He would like the Australian people to remember him as a fair-minded, talented, philosophical, true blue Aussie, but adds 'The best is yet to come.'

After photographing Jimmy in 2004 we got back in the car. As I was driving him home, he closed his eyes and sang one of Elvis's classics, 'Love me tender'. He is a very inspirational person, who always focuses on the positive things in life—something we should all try to do.

Jack Lockett

JOHN HENRY LOCKETT was born near Bendigo, Victoria on 22 January 1891. Jack, as he liked to be called, was an illegitimate child and thought that his mother was his sister until he was seven, when he found out the truth. His mother remarried and Jack received constant beatings from his alcoholic stepfather.

Jack left school when he was twelve and started work on a farm: 'I got five shillings a week to sow the crops, which was done by horses. One day when I was putting some things in the back of the truck, a horse kicked me and smashed my leg into pieces; it was three months before I could get out of the hospital bed.'

Jack enlisted in the Australian Imperial Force (AIF) on 24 March 1916; he was twenty-five. 'If you didn't go to war, you would get a white feather [to represent being a coward]. You weren't forced, but you felt like you had to go.' Lockett joined the D Company in the 38th Battalion, with the rank of private. 'As time went on they kept trying to promote me, but because I had no education, I kept denying them. I could read and write, but just to get by.' Jack ended up in France in November 1916, as part of the 10th Brigade, 3rd Division. Originally Jack's role was that of a bomb thrower, but as time passed he became a sharpshooter.

By the time Jack had returned to Australia on 5 August 1919, he had been in some horrific battles; most of them on the Western Front: 'Oh! The first three months were horrible. We spent time in the trenches, which were full of mud, and in winter the trenches would freeze and I got frostbitten feet, so I would wash them in warm water.'

Like most at war Jack was taught to hate the enemy. 'When you are in war, they feed you so much propaganda that you start to really hate the enemy. But I'll tell you this: my friends that fought in Gallipoli told me that at the end of Gallipoli, the Australians and the Turks were playing cards together!' By the end of 1917 Jack had been promoted to sergeant. In 1918 Lockett, with the 38th Battalion, saw action in Marrett Wood, Morlincourt, Proyart, Dernancourt, Bray, Suzanne, Vaux and Clary. Most of these well-known battles were very bitter but somehow

Jack survived. 'At night in the infantry, we would advance and by morning we would shell the enemy, then keep advancing; it was very organised. We would spend four days in the front line, then were given four days to rest. A lot of people were scared. You would see an officer one day and he would be gone the next. But I never thought of being killed, I mean it was in your mind, but I never thought about it, you never had time.'

After the war Jack married a girl he had met just before he had left for war. 'She was a waitress and I met her at a dance, then I enlisted; so we would write to each other, while I was fighting. I had to wait four years to get home, but when I did we got married.' After the war Jack continued to work as a farmer. Like most of us he had his ups and downs, but overall Jack Lockett had a very good and long life. When he passed away in May 2002, he was 111 years old and Australia's oldest male. In 2000 Jack was a torchbearer and carried the Olympic torch through Bendigo; he rates that day as the greatest day of his life. 'I did a good job, I was very proud of myself. There were thousands of people cheering me and a few of them had a tear in their eyes.'

When I met Jack in 2000, he was 109 and had a very sharp memory. He could still walk quite well and to me he looked and acted like a man of about 80. He had newspaper clippings of people that had passed away in Australia, that were older than him. 'I suppose being the oldest male in Australia means that I am part of history.' He was certainly part of history. Jack, reached the age of 111 and was still able to tell stories of when he was a child growing up in Australia in the 1800s.

Colleen McCullough

Author

COLLEEN MCCULLOUGH was always going to be a writer; it's just that at first she had a 'real job' that kept her from writing.

Born on 1 June 1947, Colleen was writing stories and poetry even as a small child. Practising medicine was what she desired, but medicine also had to wait. Colleen had a skin condition that prevented her from using some chemicals, in relation to cleaning her hands, which unfortunately meant that she could not continue as a medical graduate. She went instead into the science world; trained as a neurophysiologist and established the Department of Neurophysiology at Royal North Shore Hospital in Sydney. After working there for five years, Colleen moved to London where she worked in various places including the Hospital for Sick Children and the Midland Centre for Neurology and Neurosurgery.

While working in the United Kingdom she became friends with Professor Gilbert H Glaser, who was the chairman for the Department of Neurology at Yale Medical School. He was so impressed with Colleen's work that he asked her to work with him at Yale University in the United States.

Colleen packed her bags and went to Yale where she stayed for ten years. Although she enjoyed working in the medical profession, she was being paid half of what her male peers were receiving. She needed to change careers.

A highly intelligent person, who is multitalented McCullough decided to pick up a pen and paper and write a novel. In 1972 Colleen wrote her first novel *Tim*, which was a highly successful book and sold very well, both in Australia and around the world. It was made into a movie and launched a then unknown Mel Gibson's movie career. It was Colleen's second book, however, that would launch her into the stratosphere. *The Thorn Birds*, became an international bestseller, published in over twenty languages. Studio executives in the United States realised the potential of McCullough's book and paid US$1.9 million for the manuscript—a record at the time. *The Thorn Birds*, went on to become an extremely successful telemovie. Colleen McCullough was now an international star.

Colleen decided that she could no longer divide her time between writing and neurophysiology, so she left the medical profession and was welcomed with open arms by readers who eagerly awaited her next book.

After lots of media attention, Colleen wanted to relocate somewhere peaceful and away from the limelight; she found the ideal place; an island on the Pacific Ocean, called Norfolk Island. However, it took Colleen almost two years to get authorisation to live there permanently. She has lived on the island for over 20 years now and couldn't be happier, she was also lucky enough to meet her husband there.

Colleen is a member of the New York Academy of Sciences; she is a fellow of the American Association for the Advancement of Science and a patron of countless others. Colleen is a 'jack of all trades'. She has not only dabbled in countless professions; she has excelled in them.

I met Colleen McCullough in 2000. At the time I was working for Grace Bros (now Myer) in Sydney. I received a phone call at work from a friend of mine, Peter Carrette. Carrette was doing a photo shoot of McCullough for one of the British newspapers to promote her current book. Peter told me that I had to be at the hotel in the city in one hour. Luckily for me I was granted the time off so I rushed home, grabbed my camera and rushed into the city to take this shot. I was introduced to Colleen and the next thing I knew I was in a limousine sitting next to her driving down to the foreshore of Sydney Harbour. I took the photos of Colleen and asked her some questions for my research and before I knew it I was folding clothes for the rest of the afternoon. For me it was a day of rags to riches and back again, literally.

Frank McDonald

World War I and II veteran

FRANK MCDONALD was born on 26 June 1896, in, Tasmania. When war broke out in 1914 Frank tried to join the army, but was told he couldn't because he had bad teeth. He went to Queensland for two years, working as a clerk telegrapher and with the railways before going back to Tasmania to enlist in March 1916: 'It was a lot easier to join in 1916; all of our men were dying.' Frank felt it was his duty to fight for his country.

Unlike many men before him, Frank knew the dangers he was to face when he went to war. He did not sign up for an adventure, he signed up to fight. Frank joined the 40th Battalion, which was a unique unit, as it was made up entirely of Tasmanians. On 1 July 1916 the 40th battalion left Australia on the *Berrima*, arriving in England on 22 August. After training, they left for France in November 1916 and unfortunately for the 40th Battalion they had to endure one of the coldest and harshest winters in Europe's history.

In October 1917 the 40th Battalion fought in the third battle of Ypres, also referred to as Passchendaele. The Battalion had three days to walk 96km to reach Ypres, in full combat gear and rifle. On 12 October they attacked the Germans. Frank McDonald was a brave and courageous fighter that day; as the battalion continued to press forward, Frank 'displayed conspicuous gallantry and devotion to the duty in action … he did splendid work, maintaining communication lines back to headquarters', according to his medal award. And: 'The conditions were exceedingly trying owing to the station being in an area which was continuously under fire. Nevertheless, he personally saw to the maintenance of the lines, until the battalion was relieved.'

The 40th were heavily attacked and gassed; they lost 248 men, but somehow Frank survived. He was awarded the Military Medal. Frank saw and was involved in some of the fiercest and bloodiest battles in World War I.

'Once I was out preparing lines. It was dead flat country. I was tying a knot in a cable, when eight shells blew up around me, I felt the putty that I had in my pocket burn into my leg. My friend watched this and reported me dead when he went back to base. An hour later I walked in; they all looked up at me and said "You're dead!" I replied, "Not yet."'

Frank was highly skilled with a rifle. 'I practised for one year to shoot fast and straight. If I had Germans running at me, I had to be fast and accurate. I never used a bayonet. Why stab someone, when a bullet will do the same job much quicker?' Remarkably Frank was never injured at war. After the war ended he travelled around Europe, then returned to Australia in 1919. 'When we returned from World War I, Australians didn't want to know you, didn't want to talk to you. It was beneath some of them to talk to a returned soldier.'

When World War II broke out Frank was selling fridges in David Jones. He wanted to travel overseas and fight for his country, so he re-enlisted in the army. 'But the army thought I was too old for action and I served for five years at the Victoria Barracks in Sydney, doing clerical work.'

Frank McDonald passed away on 23 August 2003, aged 107. He was the last surviving decorated Australian soldier from World War I. The Military Medal is one of the highest possible medals awarded to a non-commissioned soldier, surpassed only by the Victoria Cross and the distinguished Conduct Medal. Of the 330 000 Australians who saw active service in World War I, only 3 per cent received the Military Medal. 'When all is said and done I was only one of thousands of Australians who fought during World War I. I was lucky to have come back, but I don't see what all the fuss is about.'

When I met Frank McDonald in February 2002 he was aged 106, but he could still remember places, dates and names of battlefields, towns and friends. He was one of the last of a stoic, brave generation and was proud to have represented his country in war.

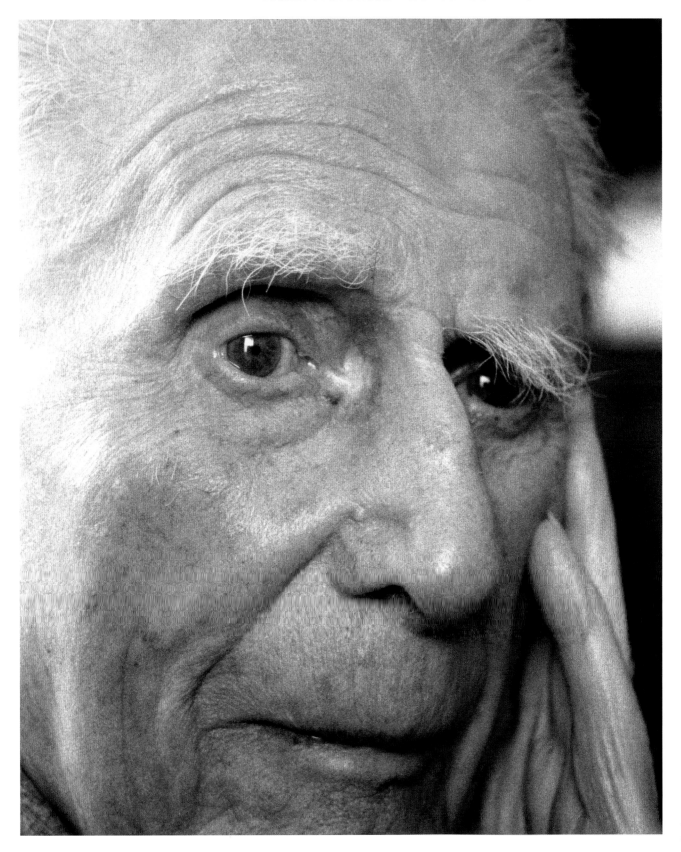

Heather McKay
Squash player

HEATHER MCKAY was born in Queanbeyan, NSW, on 31 July 1941. Heather was the eighth of 11 children to be born into the Blundell family. From an early age Heather showed tremendous hand–eye coordination, which helped her win the Queanbeyan junior tennis championship. Heather also played cricket and football with her older brothers and took a keen interest in hockey. In 1959 when Heather was on a hockey trip to Sydney with her team, she played her first game of squash. 'I took up squash to get fit for hockey. This new game of squash was supposed to get you fit for all sports.' After returning home from Sydney, two squash courts had opened near her home. She started working in the local newsagency and after work would practise and challenge other opponents.

After a short time Heather was playing and beating all of the women, so she started to challenge men. Heather was then persuaded by her practice partner, Alan Netting, to enter the NSW Country Championships in Wollongong. In April 1960 Heather won the junior final, but narrowly lost the senior tournament to top seed Evonne West. Heather then gained a place in the NSW squash team for the National Championships in Brisbane. Within a short time she had moved up in the squash ranks and was playing at state level.

In 1961 Heather won her second Australian Championship and by 1962 she was in the United Kingdom playing against the best squash players in the world. Heather won her way into the Scottish Championships final, during which she broke both of her racquets and had to borrow one from a spectator. She couldn't come back from being behind and lost to British champion Fran Marshall. This was be the last time Heather lost a game of squash in her entire career.

In the British Open Heather played against Fran Marshall again; Heather knew Marshall's game from the Scottish Championships and beat her in three straight games to win the British Open. Heather then returned to Australia, where she lived in Sydney and worked in a squash complex to make a living. She practised against the

men, one of whom was Brian McKay, an all-round sportsman and a squash coach. Heather and Brian married in 1965. Because she practised against male players, Heather's game was faster and stronger than other females; she was simply in a class of her own.

Heather McKay went on to be the worlds greatest ever female squash player, winning 16 consecutive British Open Championships (1962–77), and 14 consecutive Australian Women's Amateur Championships (1960–73). In 1975 Heather and Brian accepted a coaching job in Canada. In 1976 McKay defeated Karen Gardner in just nine minutes at the British Open and won the first Women's World Open Championship. McKay won her final British Open Championship in 1977; due to her busy load as a coach, she did not compete the following year. She won her final Women's World Open Championship in 1979, and played and won her final professional game of squash in 1981, winning the North American Open. Heather never officially announced her retirement; it was just that she was too busy coaching in Canada to compete in any more tournaments. As Heather puts it, 'I just wanted to go out on top.'

Heather was never beaten in her professional squash career, which started in 1974. Incredibly, she was also named in the Australian hockey team in 1967 and 1971, but due to her squash commitments never actually played a representative game. McKay is regarded as the world's greatest ever squash player and the American magazine *Sports Illustrated* described her record as 'unmatched by any other woman in sport'. Heather has been given numerous awards and honours including an AM and an MBE.

I met Heather in 2004 at her home in Canberra. She was very humble, friendly and generous with her time. When I asked her what made her better than the rest, she gave me this answer: 'It was a combination of a number of things that made me win so many times. I was mentally tough, very fit and a good mover. I covered the court well and hit the ball harder and with more accuracy than most of the other women.'

Gwen Meredith

Radio serial writer

GWENYTH MEREDITH was born in Orange, NSW on 18 November 1907. She completed her secondary education at Sydney Girls High School and her tertiary education at the University of Sydney, graduating with a bachelor of arts. While Gwen was at university a friend suggested that they should write a book together; she agreed and they started writing but never finished. Gwen eventually opened a bookshop, where she worked for seven years. She continued to show an interest in writing and in her late twenties another friend suggested that they should start a book club. The club members started writing plays with a young actress by the name of Gwen Plumb. Other actors joined and they started productions of small plays. Gwen Meredith wrote Plumb's first solo play *Wives Have Their Uses*, which received good reviews.

A friend informed Gwen that the ABC was running a competition and they were looking for new plays. Gwen entered and the ABC chose one of her plays to perform on radio . For Gwen it was just a hobby and at the time it was nothing that she took too seriously: 'Girls in my day were not supposed to work, but Gwen Plumb said that I should write plays for money.' Gwen married Ainsworth Harrison on Christmas Eve 1938 and during the war they moved to Melbourne. The ABC wrote to Gwen and asked her if she wanted to write a show for the radio called *The Lawsons*.

'The ABC was trying to persuade people on the land to grow more crops, such as peas and corn. It was during World War II and we had to feed a lot of Americans, as well as our own people.' The Rural Department would give Gwen ideas to incorporate into the storylines. *The Lawsons* was about a family that lived on the land and grew crops, and Gwen's creative writing encouraged farmers to be more like the characters in the serial. *The Lawsons* ran for five years. When the war finished Gwen decided that was enough writing, but the ABC persuaded her to continue. '*The Lawsons* finished on a Friday and *Blue Hills* started on the Monday. They gave me the weekend off!' *Blue Hills* started in 1949 and ran continuously on ABC radio until 1976. It is the longest running radio serial in the history of Australian radio and it launched the careers of many of Australia's actors. Gwen wrote 5795 episodes.

'During the 1950s a lot of people were immigrating to Australia. The Immigration Department asked me if I could introduce immigrants as characters into *Blue Hills*, so I went to Glasgow and learnt about their lives and background. I then came back home on a ship full of immigrants and introduced the characters from different countries into the show, so that the Australian public would accept the characters, not just in the show, but in real life. If my characters accepted them in *Blue Hills*, then so could the Australian people.'

Gwen retired in 1976 from professional writing; she received thousands of letters from the Australian public asking for more of *Blue Hills*. One letter always makes her laugh: 'A woman wrote to me just after the show had finished and said that when she heard on air that *Blue Hills* was stopping, she walked around in shock all day. In the evening the listener thought to herself; well, it's just as well Gwen stopped because she might have died while she was still writing it, then we would never have known what would've happened. I suppose that's one good reason for finishing it.' Gwen said with a laugh.

I met Gwen in 2002 at her home in Bowral; I spent the day with her and had an entertaining time with a great lady. Reflecting on *Blue Hills*, Gwen told me, '*Blue Hills* depended on characterisation. It didn't have to have a burning building at the end of every episode. I really think that the listeners were more interested in how each character would react to something.' Photos, interviews, lunch and laughter—I couldn't have asked for anything more! Well maybe one more episode of *Blue Hills*?

Keith Miller

Cricketer

IN HIS HEYDAY, Keith Miller looked more like a debonair movie star than a sportsman. Idolised by men, loved by women and feared by his opponents, Keith struck a dashing figure on the cricket pitch, whether bowling or batting. Keith could do both well. He was in the true sense of the word 'a natural'. He was a great man, never one to 'blow his own trumpet', especially in regards to his sporting achievements, which besides cricket, included 50 VFL (AFL) games for St Kilda, and named a member of the Victorian team in 1946.

Born Keith Ross Miller in November 1919, after aviators Sir Keith and Sir Ross Smith, Keith was gifted with greatness from the very beginning. When he was just eighteen he made his cricketing debut for Victoria, scoring 181 runs. But just as he was making a name for himself in Australian cricket, Keith was called off to war. Keith was a Mosquito fighter (Mosquito bombers were used by the RAAF), for five years.

His ability to play cricket was noticed while he was playing for the Australian services team in World War II. Once the war was over, Keith was named in the Australian cricket team. In 1946-7 England came out to Australia to play cricket, and Keith played a critical part in their defeat; he was second only to Bradman in batting and second to the great Lindwall in bowling. Yet the English fans loved him—he had dignity and a clear love of cricket. Keith was the post-war poster boy for England and his popularity never waned in over 50 years.

In 1948, in the second match of that year's England tour, Keith scored 202 not out against Leicestershire, and tore through the English batsmen. At the Test in Leeds, Bradman, Hassett and Morris were all out for 68. Miller, with Harvey, saved the game, which led to Australia winning every game during that tour. In fact the 1948 Australian team are still regarded as the greatest team in the history of cricket. The team are still known by their nickname, 'The Invincibles'.

Keith's statistics are great, but they are not the greatest. From 1946 to 1957 he played 55 Tests scoring 2958 runs at an average of 36.97. He bowled 170 test wickets at an average of 22.97. However, Keith never aimed for impressive statistics. But he is still highly regarded in present day cricket and in 2000 was named vice captain in the Australian Cricket Board Test Team of the Century. His most cherished award was the request for his portrait, which is hung in the prestigious Long Room at Lords. Sir Donald Bradman is the only other Australian to be granted this honour.

Keith is regarded as the greatest all-rounder to play for Australia. He will be remembered as a dashing young man who could bowl, bat and field with the very best of them. If need be, he could turn a losing game into a winning game; with his mate Ray Lindwall, they broke the opposition's batting, knocking them off, one by one.

The man nicknamed 'Nugget' for his bronzed Aussie good looks and sporting prowess, passed away on 11 October 2004, aged 84. He will be remembered just as much off the field as on. Throughout Miller's life he was immensely proud that he had served in World War II for his country and we as a nation are proud to call him one of our own.

I met Keith Miller a number of times at his house in the northern beaches suburb of Narrabeen. He and his wife were always very welcoming; he used to joke that he married her because she was American and didn't know anything about cricket! That's the sort of bloke he was. He made me feel, like I was one of his mates. He was one of those few people that no matter how many words you use to describe them, you just can't. He had that magic 'something'.

George Moore

Jockey

IMAGINE BEING an athlete and winning 2277 races. Well, that's exactly what jockey George Moore achieved. George was born in Queensland in 1923. As a child he was interested in horses and at just 14 he was an apprentice to Queensland trainer Louis Dahl. George first raced at Albion Park and within a short time became a successful apprentice rider. He decided that to further his career he had to relocate to Sydney, where he could get better rides and greater prize money.

Ironically things were about to get worse before they got better. In a race at Canterbury, Moore had a bad fall and broke his leg. He had ridden the horse as a favour for a friend, when he could have easily ridden the winner. Moore learnt a valuable lesson from that ride: winning was the name of the game. While he was injured, Sydney's top trainers all but forgot about George Moore and on his return to the track he discovered it would be almost impossible to get a ride in the city. So he sought work in country centres, where his ability was instantly obvious, and once again he became very successful. George was also able to fine-tune his skills at these country meets.

After returning to Sydney, George met with leading trainer TJ Smith. Tommy Smith happened to be a great admirer of George's and asked the jockey to ride for him. This would become a turning point for both George and TJ's personal and professional lives. In 1949 George rode Playboy, trained by Smith, and won the Australian Jockey Club Derby. From that day on George never looked back. By 1956 he had 1040 wins in 3403 rides; in the same period his nearest rival had 426 wins, from 4263 rides. George was a punter's dream and a bookie's nightmare.

In 1957 George pursued his racing career overseas. After winning his first of eight successive Sydney Jockey Premierships (ten in total), George challenged his European counterparts, winning on Taboun in the 1959 English Two Thousand Guineas, as well as the Prix de l'Arc de Triomphe on Saint Crespin. The following year George won the French Derby on Charlottsville.

George divided his time between Sydney and Europe, winning almost every important race that he entered. In 1967 George won the English Derby (Royal Palace) and in the same year, while racing in England, George won the 1000 and 2000 Guineas.

George was considered by many in England the greatest jockey they had ever seen. Historians write that no-one could see an opportunity like George could—his horse would race past his opponents and to the amazement of others, somehow find a gap. He had a profound gift with horses, considering them highly intelligent beings. This gift led him to the top of his profession around the world, and he won races in Australia, New Zealand, England, Ireland, Germany, France and America. He was undisputedly in a class of his own.

Tulloch was George's most famous mount. From 1957 George rode Tulloch to victory in the derbies in New South Wales, Victoria and Queensland, the Victoria St Leger and the Queen Elizabeth Stakes. At the Victoria Derby Tulloch took seconds off Phar Lap's record for that race. George considered Tulloch the best horse he had ever ridden. Incredibly, though he won almost every major race that the world had to offer, George never won the Melbourne Cup.

After two serious falls in 1969, where George broke his collarbone, finger, five ribs, pelvis and suppressed two vertebrae in his neck, he went into semi-retirement and was never able to regain his full strength. He finally retired from racing in 1971. Considered by many, to be the world's greatest jockey, George rode five winners in one day on five occasions. In 1969 at the Easter racing carnival, he rode 15 winners over four days.

After retiring, George successfully trained horses in France before relocating to Hong Kong.

I met George in 2002 at his penthouse, which overlooks Surfers Paradise beach in Queensland. He was a quiet, introverted and particularly modest man who was more excited about showing my friend and me his 180 degree view of the beach than talking about himself and his astonishing racing career.

Rupert Murdoch

Keith Rupert Murdoch was born on 11 March 1931 in Melbourne. Rupert looked up to his father Keith, who started out as a reporter then became an advisor to former prime minister Billy Hughes. Keith Murdoch became Australia's most influential newspaper executive and owner of *The Adelaide* newspaper. Rupert studied at Oxford University in the United Kingdom, where he felt free from his influential family, but his freedom was dramatically cut short when his father died in 1952. As the only son, Rupert flew back to Australia and took control of the small Adelaide newspaper.

Rupert was an aggressive entrepreneur; his strategy was to buy struggling newspapers and turn them into profitable ones. In 1961 Rupert purchased Festival Records which at the time was almost bankrupt. Rupert soon turned Festival Records into the top local recording company. In 1999 Rupert bought Mushroom Records and merged Mushroom and Festival into one company (Festival Mushroom Records).

Over the next ten years Rupert continued to expand his empire, first by buying up publications, then by breaking into television by purchasing a television station in Wollongong. During the 1970s Rupert was buying newspapers and magazines in the United Kingdom, including *News of the World* and the slow-selling *Sun*. Rupert introduced the 'page 3 girl' in *The Sun* and completely changed the format of the newspaper, doubling its circulation within months. In the United States he bought the *New York Post* and other publications. In 1987 he purchased the Australian Herald and Weekly Times Ltd, the corporation that his father Keith had once managed. With his publications Rupert could make or break a politician, and many politicians became friendly with him so that he would favour them in his publications. In doing so Rupert could influence the public in their voting decisions. Rupert is commonly known as the single most politically significant media owner in the world.

Rupert continued to expand his business and bought 20th Century Fox and Fox TV. Due to his ownership of Fox, Rupert had to become an American citizen in 1985: there is legislation in the United States that stipulates only US citizens can own American television stations. In 1993 Rupert bought STAR, a satellite TV company. The potential was huge, with prospective audiences from Japan to the Middle East. The only problem was that Japan and other countries didn't have satellite dishes and the company could not expand. It was the early 1990s. Rupert had been on a spending spree, but the recession had hit and the company was in danger of collapsing. Luckily for Rupert the banks believed in him and did not foreclose on his loans.

News Corporation bounced back and by the mid 1990s Rupert was again one of the most powerful and successful medial moguls of the world. Today aged 74, Rupert is still the CEO of News Corporation Ltd and owns numerous newspapers, magazines, publishing houses, cable networks, television and movie studios and even the LA Dodgers baseball team. Rupert has come a long way since he acquired a small newspaper in Adelaide; he is regarded as one of the greatest business minds of the world. Rupert is the only media tycoon to have formed and managed a genuinely worldwide media empire. Today he still lobbies for the cross-media ownership laws in Australia to be changed, which have frustratingly evaded him.

I had wanted to photograph Murdoch for some time but had no idea how to meet him. In 2002 I went down to the Rushcutters Bay Marina, where the Sydney to Hobart boats were preparing to leave. Murdoch's son Lachlan was racing that year and Rupert was there to wish his son good luck. After father and son said goodbye, I approached Murdoch and told him I was putting together a book about Australian legends. 'I'm not an Australian legend,' replied a surprised Murdoch. 'I think you are and so do a lot of other people.' 'OK then, what can I do for you?' asked Murdoch. 'I would like to take some photos of you for the book.' 'Take two,' he replied. I took two photos and he was off. 'Good luck' he said as he moved away. There's no wasting time with Rupert Murdoch.

Kel Nagle

Golfer

K EL NAGLE was born in Sydney on 21 December 1920. When Nagle was 16 he found a job as an apprentice carpenter. 'I was working for a builder wheeling barrels of bricks and cement about. One day it was very hot, so I sat down to have a break. When I sat down and watched the tiler tile the roof, the boss came over and screamed, "What are you doing?" I told him I was watching the tiler. The boss said, "It's a pity you didn't do a bit more work." I felt like throwing the cement barrel at him. I got on my bike and left. I then started working at Pymble Golf Club, and it was the best thing that ever happened to me.'

Kel started out as a caddy, then worked in the golf shop. Kel couldn't play golf, so he had to start from scratch. As time passed, Kel's game improved. He started playing in local tournaments and was doing very well. Just as he was starting to make a name for himself World War II broke out and Kel spent four and a half years in the army. Like many of his era, Kel's profession was interrupted by the war. After returning from military duties he took up golf again. In 1949, three years after he had turned professional, Kel won the Australian PGA title. He decided to try his luck in England in 1959, but he did not do as well as expected, so he returned to Sydney, where he became the pro at Pymble Golf Club. This gave Kel plenty of time to perfect his game; he shortened his swing and taught himself to hit the ball straighter.

By 1960 Kel was 40 years old and was playing the best golf of his life. He went overseas with his good friend Peter Thompson—they played in numerous tournaments in the United States and came third in the Canada Cup (World Cup) that year, having won it in 1954 and 1959.

'Peter Thompson said to me, "You're playing really well, I think you're going to win the British Open." "No, I don't think so," I told him, but Peter was convinced. He said, "You're driving well, putting well, you're ready." Thompson told Kel that they would practise together at St Andrews. Thompson showed Kel the traps of the course and felt that Kel was going to win.

The year 1960 was important for the British Open—it was the centenary year. Kel felt confident about his game—he was on 35/1 to win. Thompson was so confident that Kel was going to win that he put a bet on the game. Kel started the tournament very well and was up against rising star Arnold Palmer. Kel did not let Thompson down; by the final day it was Kel against Palmer. By the eighteenth hole, both players were neck and neck. Palmer sank a birdie, which put pressure on Kel. But Kel then sank a 10-foot putt on the seventeenth and a par on the eighteenth to win the game. At the age of forty, Kel had won the prestigious British Open. In 1964 he won the Canadian Open, and went on to win the Australian PGA six times, the New Zealand Open seven times, and the New Zealand PGA nine times.

After many years on the professional circuit, Kel entered the seniors' tournament. He won the British senior title in 1973 and 1975 and the World Seniors Titles in 1971 and 1975. 'I actually won more money in the seniors' tournaments than I won in the professional tournaments,' he says. At the end of Kel's career he had won fifty-five major tournaments. 'I still like to watch golf on television and I like to watch the women's tournaments. They have got some great players at the moment, but I have to say that Tiger Woods is the best player that I have ever seen; he's got the complete game.'

I met Nagle in 2000 after a friendly phone call inviting me over to his house in Sydney. We did some shots at the back of his house, which amusingly looked like a golf course. He was a very kind and unassuming person who showed tremendous interest in the golfers of today.

Sir Marcus Oliphant
Scientist/State governor

MARCUS LAURENCE ELWIN OLIPHANT was born on 8 October 1901 in Adelaide. As a child, Oliphant was interested in science and when he was 14, Mark (as he liked to be called) was experimenting with fireworks in his house and the fireworks exploded—he nearly lost his eyes. However, this accident did not deter Oliphant from science. Once he had completed school, he attended Adelaide University and graduated with honours in 1927. He then went to Cambridge where he studied under the famous Lord Rutherford of New Zealand, who was the director of the Cavendish Laboratory at Cambridge University.

In 1932, the Cavendish Laboratory split the atom by artificially accelerating particles; the centre where Sir Marcus worked was a world leader in experimental physics. Sir Marcus became Cavendish Laboratory's Assistant Director of Research in 1935 and worked on nuclear disintegration. He then began to concentrate on the design of heavy high voltage apparatus and was able to produce intense beams of protons and of the nuclei of heavy hydrogen. Sir Marcus also worked with lithium nuclei, which he separated into two lithium isotopes by electromagnetic means. Oliphant discovered new forms of Hydrogen (Deuterium and Tritium) and Helium (Helium 3); discoveries which laid the foundation for the development of nuclear weapons.

In 1937, Sir Marcus was Poynting Professor of Physics at the University of Birmingham. Here, he established a nuclear physics research program. Under his direction the laboratory was responsible for one of the most significant scientific inventions of the war, the resonator magnetron. The magnetron revolutionised radar and was described by US publication *Scientists at War* as 'the most important contribution of reverse lend lease'. Emitted in pulses of intense force it could search for ships and submarines. For the first time this ingenious invention allowed air force bomber pilots to identify their targets with confidence.

In 1943, Sir Marcus went to the United States to share his knowledge of nuclear physics and to explore the possibilities of radar. While in North America he ended up working on the Manhattan Project. The project involved a number of brilliant scientists who created what we know today as the atomic bomb.

The atomic bombs were later dropped on Hiroshima and Nagasaki in 1945, ending World War II. Sir Marcus was so appalled about these bombs that he perceived himself as a war criminal, even though he hadn't known what the bombs were intended for. For the rest of his life, Sir Marcus campaigned vigorously for the non-violent use of atomic energy and spoke out against all nuclear weapons. He was devastated that he had played a role in developing weapons, which had destroyed so many people's lives.

In 1950 Sir Marcus returned to Australia to become Director of the Research School of Physical Sciences at the Australian National University. He headed the university's research unit on ionised gases and served as chairman of a committee that advised the government on the development of nuclear power stations; he also became the founding president of the Australian Academy of Sciences.

In 1971, Sir Marcus, aged seventy, chose another career; he was appointed governor of South Australia, a position that he proudly held until 1976. The people of South Australia welcomed Sir Marcus with open arms and he was a much-loved governor of the state. After retiring from politics, Oliphant continued to campaign against the use of nuclear weapons. He was an inspiration to many scientists around the world, and to all of those who oppose nuclear weapons. Sir Marcus would later say: 'I am one of those persons who wish the atomic weapons had never been made.' In 1959 he was named a Knight of the British Empire and in 1977 he was awarded the Order of Australia.

I met Sir Marcus Oliphant on 11 July 2000 in hospital. I photographed him while he was resting in his bed; he passed away three days later aged 98 on 14 July 2000. His daughter Vivian wanted Sir Marcus to be represented in this book and I give my thanks to her and the family for their cooperation.

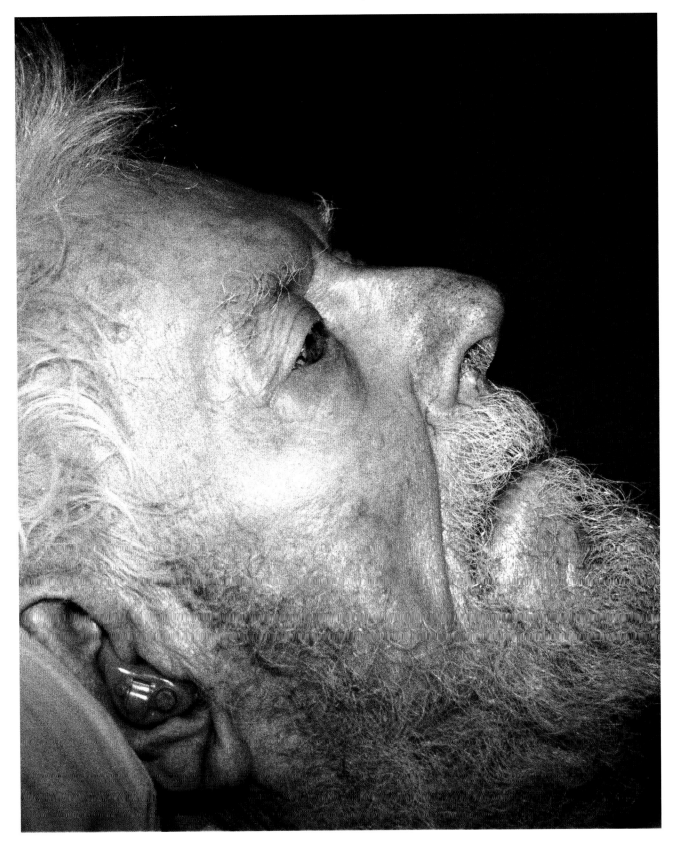

Margaret Olley

Artist

MARGARET HANNAH OLLEY was born in Brisbane in 1923. After completing her schooling she travelled to Sydney where she attended East Sydney Technical College Art School. Like most young struggling artists, Margaret had to find a way of making a living while studying. She found a job painting theatre props, and discovered that she was very talented at designing wallpaper. In 1945 Margaret left Australia for Paris where she continued to study art and pursued her talent for wallpaper designing.

In 1947, Margaret was back in Sydney and attended an exhibition dressed in a very unusual outfit. It was an old wedding dress combined with some parachute silk and a large straw hat. Margaret certainly stood out from the crowd! After the exhibition Margaret and a few other artists ended up at Russell Drysdale's house partying the night away. They eventually ended up at Vaucluse House, where they watched the sun rise. After the 'all nighter' fellow artist William Dobell (who was a very well known and established artist of the day) and Margaret caught the tram home together. It was during the ride home that Dobell asked Margaret to sit for him. Margaret agreed and she sat for Dobell, still wearing her eye-catching dress.

In 1948, Dobell entered the portrait of Margaret into the Archibald Prize and won. Ironically Dobell was not going to enter the painting as he did not like it, but he was convinced to enter it by fellow artist Sali Herman. Fourteen thousand people viewed the painting on the first weekend of the exhibition, giving Margaret tremendous exposure and publicity. She was a known artist before Dobell's winning portrait, but now she became a household name. That very same year Margaret held her first solo exhibition, which was extremely successful. The Art Gallery of New South Wales and the National Gallery of Victoria both purchased her work.

Since her first exhibition in 1948, Margaret has had over fifty solo exhibitions. She paints mainly objects that decorate her distinctive Paddington home, generally fruits and flowers or anything else that she has managed to collect while travelling around the world. Even though the subjects of her work are not unique, Margaret's work is instantly recognisable due to her almost magical ability to capture both colour and light.

Margaret's work has become highly sought after, not only in Australia but in London, where collectors are more than willing to pay for an Olley masterpiece. Margaret has not been affected by fame or wealth and donates a lot of money and her personal time to art students and galleries. In one instance Edmund Capon, who is the director of the Art Gallery of NSW, rang Margaret to ask if she could help in the purchasing of a Cezanne drawing, which was to be auctioned. Capon was hoping Margaret might help in purchasing one of the master's drawings. Margaret, without thinking twice, wrote a cheque for $250 000. Capon eventually ended up buying three of Cezanne's drawings. Margaret was awarded the Order of Australia in 1991.

Since 1999 I have been fortunate enough to visit Margaret at her Paddington home in Sydney a number of times. When you enter her house, it's like stepping into one of her paintings, a dreamlike experience. Margaret is just as famous for being eccentric as she is for being a philanthropist and a painter (as she prefers to be called, rather than an artist). There is no-one else quite like her.

Earl Owen

Microsurgeon

WHERE DO you start with somebody who seems to have achieveded the impossible? Earl Owen was born in Sydney on 6 September 1933. Earl's father, a doctor, gave him a small doctor's badge and bag and called Earl his little assistant, taking him to visit his patients. Earl's mother was an opera singer, so he grew up surrounded by medicine and music. Earl began to play the piano at age five.

At Cranbrook School in Sydney Earl carved figurines out of balsa wood with his Swiss army knife inside his desk. Creating a whole army, he ended up with a battleground on a bed of plasticine without the teacher's knowledge. Earl would directly look at the teacher, with his school books on the desktop, while his hands sculpted inside his desk. He did this for a full year, maybe training himself subconsciously as a surgeon. When the teacher found out, Earl was taken to the headmaster; however, the headmaster 'punished' him in an unusual way. Realising Earl had talent, his punishment was to carve the school's crest for his office, where it hung for years.

At 14, Earl won a piano competition and the following year he played for famed pianist Solomon, who was then a visiting maestro. Impressed by Earl's talent Solomon invited the teenager to study under his supervision.

Earl accepted, however, he also wanted to pursue a medical career. Solomon told Earl that he should concentrate on one or the other. Earl went to Sydney University, graduating in medicine in 1958. After working at the Royal Prince Alfred Hospital, where he had already started research work, he did a year in Melbourne's Alfred Hospital as a trainee surgeon, still longing for music and wanting to go to London to do both.

From 1961 to 1969 Earl worked in London as a senior registrar at Great Ormond Street Hospital for Sick Children, obtaining his higher degrees and researching what would later be called microsurgery. He went across to Germany in 1965 to work with Zeiss (microscope makers), who helped him design the motorised micro instruments he would need for his ground-breaking microsurgery. From 1965 to 1969 he pioneered new operations on babies with abnormalities.

Owen returned to Australia and began work at the Royal Alexandra Hospital for Children (now at Westmead), where one of his patients was a two-year-old boy whose finger had been completely severed and brought in a plastic bag. Owen contacted his superiors and explained that he believed he could successfully reattach the finger. This theory was greeted as nonsense: 'Surgery like that has never been done before and you should not proceed with the operation.' However, Owen believed in himself and with his brother-in-law assisting, forged ahead with this pioneering surgery. The following morning that first finger was working, but instead of Owen being congratulated, he was dismissed for insubordination. Fortunately for Earl, the Prince of Wales Hospital was building a children's surgery unit and the professor there was willing to take Earl on.

Owen performed many microsurgical world firsts, such as reversing vasectomies, reversing women's tubal sterilisation, and reconstructive surgery on premature babies. His hobbies include design; he designed the seating now in the Sydney Opera House, for the Fairfax boardroom, and for people with backache. 'I've always been interested in looking at things and seeing how they can be done better, so if I'm sitting in an uncomfortable seat I think of how I can improve the seat then redesign it on anatomical principles.'

On 23 September 1998, Owen and his team performed the world's first hand transplant using a hand from a deceased man. On 13 January 2000 the same team performed the world's first successful double hand transplant.

I have met Professor Owen a few times over the years and he has spent many of his precious hours with me, giving me more than enough of his time and energy for this book, and also giving me advice and perspective on a personal level. Like thousands of people around the world, I cannot thank him enough. Thank you, gracias, merci.

Michael Pate

Actor/director

Few actors in the world can boast that they have starred alongside many of Hollywood's greatest names, such as Randolph Scott, Glenn Ford, James Mason, Audrey Hepburn, Tony Curtis and John Wayne to name but a few. But Michael Pate can.

Michael Pate was born in Sydney in 1920. At the age of 18 Michael wrote and hosted a program for ABC Radio called *Youth Speaks*. This was his first taste of show business. Michael began writing for newspapers and magazines and the following year in 1939 he starred in *Lux Radio Theatre*. Michael's first big break came when the legendary Charles Chauvel cast him to perform in *Forty Thousand Horsemen*.

When World War II broke out in 1939 Michael signed up for the Australian Army in the SWPA unit. Later he was in the 1st Australian Army Amenities Entertainment Unit. After the war Michael starred in various radio plays and serials. Following a few years of doing radio, Michael realised that he needed to expand his career into the movies. In 1949 Michael was cast in the Australian movie *Sons of Matthew* and in 1950 he appeared in *Bitter Springs*.

Michael, who was not content with acting, produced, wrote, directed and adapted plays for the theatre and radio. By 1950 he had two plays showing around Australia, one of which was called *Bonaventure*. It was because of this play that Hollywood came looking for him. In 1950 one of Hollywood's largest studios, Universal Pictures, asked Michael to do a film version of his play. It was released in 1951 as *Thunder on the Hill* and starred Claudette Colbert.

Michael felt that it was time to leave Australia where he had become a household name and have a go at the American market. It didn't take long for the Hollywood studios to realise that Michael had talent. In 1953 Michael was cast in *Hondo*, playing an American Indian opposite Hollywood legend John Wayne; it was this role that most people remember him for. The following year Michael starred in Ian Fleming's television adaptation of his first tale about James Bond, *Casino Royale*. Michael became the very first actor to play the role of CIA agent Felix Leiter. This show was made into a movie, 13 years later starring David Niven and John Huston.

Michael lived in the United States for almost twenty years. He had a long and successful career in Hollywood, appearing in over fifty feature films and guest starring in over 300 television shows. While in Hollywood he also began to teach acting and lecturing on acting for film. Michael continued to act, not only on the silver screen and television, but also in the theatre, where he starred in a US version of his *Lux Radio Theatre* show, that was hosted by Cecil B. De Mille. Michael also collaborated on movie scripts for Hollywood, such as *Escape from Fort Bravo* (1953) and *Dangerous Man Alive* (1961).

Michael returned to Australia in 1968 where he was the associate producer for Norman Lindsay's *Age of Consent*. He continued to produce a wide range of shows for all three major networks and his *Maggie* show won two Gold Logies for the Seven Network. He also produced many variety shows for UNICEF. In 1971 Michael starred in the Australian television series *Matlock Police*; he stayed with the highly successful show for four years. In 1979 he wrote, produced and made his directorial debut with the adaptation of Colleen McCullough's classic novel *Tim*. It won Michael the Best Screenplay Award from the Australian Writers Guild; the movie went onto become a classic and launched a very young Mel Gibson onto the world's stage.

Michael Pate worked and became friends with some of the biggest names in Hollywood's history and became a Hollywood legend himself.

I have been exceptionally fortunate to have formed a friendship with Michael Pate during the many occasions that I have been to interview and photograph him at his Sydney home and later on at his farm. He is always very generous, and very entertaining, especially with his stories of Hollywood in the 1950s and 1960s.

Keith Payne

Vietnam War veteran VC

Iт's 24 May 1969. Keith Payne is 35 and fighting in Kon Tum Province in Vietnam. He's an officer commanding the 212th Company of 1st Mobile Strike Force. Suddenly he and his company are attacked by the enemy from three different directions. The battalion has become isolated and they are under heavy attack by mortars, rockets, grenades and artillery, all aiming in his and his soldiers' direction. Keith has been wounded in the hands and arms and it seems like his entire company is going to be wiped out …

Born in Queensland on 30 August 1933, Keith went to Ingham State School and then took an apprentice as cabinetmaker. Frustrated with his trade, Keith enlisted in the Australian Army on 13 August 1951. He served in Korea with the 1st Battalion from April 1952 until March 1953. In 1965 Keith was promoted to Warrant Officer II and later to Sergeant Major of the Officer Training Unit at Schyeville, NSW. From February 1967 until March 1968 Keith served in Papua New Guinea with the 2nd Battalion Pacific Islands Regiment as Regimental Duty Warrant Officer. In February 1969, Keith was posted as Company Commander of the 212th Company in Vietnam, their job was to stop the enemy's reinforcements and supplies moving into Vietnam.

On 24 May 1969, Keith, with his company, was caught in a vicious battle with the Vietnamese. Keith literally put himself on the line; he directly exposed himself to the enemy and in front of a full enemy attack ran from one position to another throwing grenades and firing at the enemy. Keith and the rest of the company were outnumbered and those who could retreat did. However, many of the soldiers had been wounded and were lying in the field, which was occupied by the enemy. Keith selflessly continued to attack the enemy and when night fell, knowing that the enemy still occupied the area, crawled out on his hands and knees and in the darkness of the night spent three hours saving 40 injured men. Keith finally made it back to the defensive perimeter only to find that it had gone. He then single-handedly led the injured battalion back through the enemy-occupied area and finally back to the safety of the battalion base.

Keith was sent home in 1969 due to illness and on his return was welcomed with open arms by the people of Brisbane—then being admitted to an army hospital. On 13 March 1975, Keith was discharged from the army at his own request. However, he did see further action as a captain with the army of the Sultan of Oman in the Dhofar War. When Keith returned home to Australia, he became very committed to the veterans society, and especially to sufferers of post-traumatic stress disorders

For his heroic actions in Vietnam, Warrant Officer II Keith Payne was awarded the Victoria Cross, which was presented to him by Queen Elizabeth II on board the royal yacht *Britannia* in Brisbane on 15 April 1970. He was also presented with the Distinguished Service Cross and the Silver Star by the United States and the Cross of Gallantry by The Republic of South Vietnam. Keith has had many more prestigious awards presented to him, and his portrait is displayed in the Hall of Valour at the Australian War Memorial, and his photo and citation are displayed in the Hall of Heroes at the John F Kennedy Centre in North Carolina, USA.

In 2000 Keith, along with two other Victoria Cross recipients, was honoured by Australia Post through a release of 'For Valour' stamps to commemorate their heroic achievements.

I met Keith Payne in October 2004. With a bit of luck and a lot of formula one driving I made it to his hotel in Sydney , just as he was walking out of the lift. This was a great day for me, as I had been intending to travel to Mackay in North Queensland to photograph him.

Des Renford

DES RENFORD was born in Waverley, Sydney in 1927. He showed ability in the pool by winning the state swimming championship in the 55 yards before his tenth birthday. He continued to compete in swimming races until his teenage years, when he chose to rescue people as a lifeguard, instead of racing others. Renford left the water for a few years and spent some years working as a racehorse owner, butcher, publican and alderman, but it was swimming that challenged him.

In 1967 Des went back to the pool and became interested in marathon swimming. By the following year he had finished third in a forty-kilometre race across Port Victoria's Phillip Bay. Eager to do better, Des won his first marathon on the Murray River, swimming sixty-five kilometres in 1969. After conquering the shores of Australia, Des wanted to push the boundaries a little further. In 1970 at the age of 43, Des decided to swim the English Channel, 35km between France and England. Des completed the swim, but wanted more. He decided that he wanted to be 'King of the Channel', but fellow competitor Mike Read of England also wanted the title. The pair's rivalry became more famous than their actual swims. One of Des's swims finished in gale force winds and on another he was run over by a hovercraft, luckily surviving to reach France.

By 1975, Des had swum the English Channel seven times, giving him the title of King of the Channel. Every time Des crossed the freezing waters Read followed; by 1978 Des had a 13 to 11 lead over Read. Des wanted to retire with the most swims of the Channel; he swam three more crossings and went back to Australia. Read also swam three crossings: Des had 16 successful swims to Read's 14. Des, now an international celebrity and King of the Channel, could not sit at home and rest on his laurels. By 28 October 1979, Read had swum the English Channel seventeen times, overtaking Des's record by one. The following year in 1980 Des came out of retirement and swam the Channel three times and took the record back. Des was then happy to retire once again as King of the Channel. By 1980 Des had successfully swum an amazing 19 English channels from 19 attempts.

In 1978 Des was inducted into the International Hall of Fame in the United States, becoming the first and only Australian marathon swimmer to do so. He received the Member of the British Empire (MBE) by Her Majesty Queen Elizabeth II in 1976 and went on to make two award-winning documentaries: *King of the Channel* and *Iron Man of the Sea*. Des also released his autobiography in 1992 and served as a member of the Victor Chang Cardiac Research Institutes Appeal Committee, as he had had a personal struggle with heart conditions over the years and wanted to raise awareness and funds for research.

Des kindly donated his time to both the Special Olympics and to his treasured Coffee Club, which he had formed to give people of all swimming abilities the chance to swim and then connect over a cup of coffee together. Overall, Des received hardly any acknowledgement for his sacrifices in one of the toughest, most gruelling, mentally and physically demanding sports there is.

In December 1999 Des Renford was doing his usual early morning swimming at Heffron Pool, when he had a massive heart attack. He died on 31 December 1999. On 1 March 2000 Heffron Pool was renamed The Des Renford Aquatic Centre, in honour of its famous swimmer.

I met Des Renford in 1999 on a cold and grey early morning at Heffron Pool. It was the crack of dawn and Des was the first one to arrive for his swim. We did the photo shoot and had a chat on the swimming blocks about his remarkable life. Des remarked that 'nothing great is easy'; it was a quote from the world's first successful Channel swimmer Matthew Webb, who had swum the English Channel in 1875. It was also the name of Des's autobiography—Des had lived by that quote his entire life.

Lionel Rose

Boxer

LIONEL ROSE was born on 21 June 1948. He grew up in a town near Drouin, Victoria, with his eight brothers and sisters. Rose's family were impoverished and lived in a one-room shack, with a single light and a sack filled with flour; which hung from the ceiling. Lionel and his brothers would use the flour bag as a punching bag. When Lionel was ten he made a trip to Melbourne. The trip was sponsored by a local charity to give children a few days holiday in a big city.

On his trip to Melbourne Lionel started talking to a photographer. He told the photographer that he wanted to see a professional fight, so that night Lionel and the photographer went to see George Bracken fight. Bracken was also Aboriginal, and was currently Lightweight Champion of Australia. From then on, every time Bracken fought in Victoria, Lionel would hitch a ride and watch the fight.

When Lionel turned 12, the photographer gave him his first pair of boxing gloves and Lionel started training. Lionel knew that he wanted to become the champion of the world. At 14 he left school and started working in a local saw mill to support his family, as his father had died. He continued to box and at the age of fifteen the locals at the Warragal Hotel rounded up some money and sent him off to Tasmania, where he won the Amateur Flyweight title.

Lionel was beaten by Billy Booth in a fight that decided who would represent Australia at the 1964 Olympic Games, and his coach convinced him to turn professional. Lionel agreed and moved to Melbourne, where he teamed up with Jack Rennie. After a short time Lionel moved into Rennie's house; Rennie was like a father to him. The Rennies brought Lionel up as one of their own. Jack's wife, Shirley, enrolled Lionel in English and mathematics. Lionel and Rennie were the perfect partnership: Rennie was a brilliant coach and Lionel was a gifted boxer. Lionel then started to work in a spraypainting factory and in his spare time he trained.

Lionel had his first fight against Mario Magreiss, and he won. On 11 December 1967, he fought Rocky Gattellari at the Sydney Stadium. Lionel won the fight—and sent Gattellari to hospital after knocking him out. In 1968 the World Bantamweight Title was up for grabs; the defender, 'Fighting' Harada, was going to fight Mexico's number one boxer Jesus Pimental, but Pimental asked for too much money and the promoters thought Lionel would be a cheap and easy fight for Harada.

On 27 February 1968 in Tokyo, Lionel was definitely the underdog, but like a true champion he won the Bantamweight Champion of the World. On his return home to Melbourne 250 000 people lined the streets, as Lionel drove from the airport to the Town Hall. When he arrived 10 000 people were chanting his name. In a very short time Lionel had gone from punching a bag of flour to punching his name into the record books.

Lionel successfully defended his title in March 1968, beating Alan Rudkin from England. On 2 July he beat Takao Sakurai in Tokyo and on 6 December Lionel defended his title against Chucho Castillo in Los Angeles. While in Los Angeles Lionel received a message from a friend that Elvis Presley wanted to meet him. Lionel put on his best suit and went to meet the King: 'Elvis is the King. He was a gentleman—he called me Mr Rose and was excited to meet me!'

Lionel also started a singing career, appearing on the television show *Sunny Side Up*, where he sang 'Pick Me Up on Your Way Down'. With a music career, fame and fortune Lionel lost his title on the 22 August 1969 to Rubin Olivares. In 1970 Lionel retired from boxing and released the hit single 'I Thank You'. Lionel had won 42 from 53 professional fights and was unbeaten in 22 fights from 13 May 1966 to 11 June 1969. He received an MBE and became the first Aboriginal to be named Australian of the Year in 1968.

I met Lionel in 2002, after many years trying to track him down. I took him out the back of his apartment and we did some great photos. After the photos, for a bit of fun my friend and I threw a few punches with Lionel. One of Lionel's punches broke through my friend's defence and gave him a black eye! Lionel had not lost any of his skill or power.

Murray Rose

Swimmer

IAIN MURRAY ROSE was born in England on 6 January 1939. He celebrated his first birthday coming through the Sydney Heads. In fact you could say that Murray Rose found his sea legs, whilst entering Sydney Harbour. Eight months later he was dogpaddling at Rose Bay's Redleaf Pool. By the age of five Murray Rose had his very own swimming coach, Richard Eve. Eve knew what it took to win; he had won a gold medal at the 1924 Paris Olympic Games. By the age of seven Murray was being coached by Sam Herford. Murray was a naturally gifted swimmer and with the guidance of Herford, Murray perfected his skills.

Murray continued to win numerous swimming events and was nicknamed 'the seaweed streak' due to his unusual diet, which consisted of vegetarian meals with seaweed. When Murray was 17 he was chosen for the 1956 Melbourne Olympic Games. Murray's first event was the 8 x 200 metres relay; Murray swam the third leg and Australia won gold. The very next day Murray swam in the 400 metres freestyle final. At the halfway mark, Murray saw an opportunity and broke away. He won his second gold medal in as many days, breaking the Olympic record and winning the race by six metres. Murray was the first Australian to win the 400 metres freestyle at an Olympic event and instantly became a household name.

Three days later, Murray swam in the 1500 metres freestyle final. Before the event, all four freestyle events had been won by Australia. Murray was nervous as he and the rest of the swimming team wanted an Australian clean sweep. The stadium was packed with spectators, including Prime Minister Robert Menzies. Murray had two main threats: America's Breem who had broken the world record in qualifying and Japan's Yamanaka. Just before Murray hit the water, he received a note from his coach reminding him that the time was right and to remember the basics. Murray hit the water with the whole of Australia cheering him on; the 17-year-old was under enormous pressure. Halfway through the race Yamanaka slowed and Murray made a break. Breem couldn't keep up with Murray and although Yamanaka made another attempt towards the end, Murray hung on and won the race by six metres. He became the youngest swimmer in history to win three gold medals at one Olympic Games.

Murray was part of the 1960 Australian swimming team for the Rome Olympics; he successfully defended his 400 metre crown, but was beaten by fellow Australian John Konrads in the 1500 metres, winning silver. Murray also collected a bronze in the 4 x 200 metres freestyle. After the 1960 Olympic Games, Murray needed a break from swimming. He left Australia to study in America—because of his good looks and amazing talent he was dubbed the golden boy of swimming and Hollywood came calling. Murray appeared in quite a few movies and Columbia Pictures offered Murray a seven-year movie deal, but he turned it down. After a break from the pool Murray was back in the water for the 1962 Perth Commonwealth Games where he won four gold medals.

In 1964 Murray broke the world records for the 800 metres and the 1500 metres at the US National Championships. Murray thought that he was ready for the 1964 Tokyo Olympic Games; however, without his knowledge, Australia had their team trials while he was studying in the United States. Although Murray had broken two world records that very same year, he was left out of the Australian Olympic Team, thanks to sheer bureaucracy. Murray was denied the chance to defend his titles. It's scandalous that Murray Rose wasn't given the same treatment that Ian Thorpe received for the 2004 Athens Olympic Games. We can only wonder what would of happened if he had been allowed to compete in 1964.

Murray then spent thirty years working in America as a successful executive. He worked in television in the United States and Australia, returning home in the 1990s.

I met Rose in 2004 at Redleaf Pool. It brought back childhood memories for Murray, as he had learnt to swim there. Murray has an undeniable humility and grace about him and I appreciated the time he gave me. There was definitely no ego with this true Golden Boy.

Bill Roycroft

Equestrian

BILL ROYCROFT was born James William Roycroft in March 1915. Young Bill was raised in Flowerdale and learnt to ride a horse around the same time as he learnt to walk. As a child he use to ride his horse to school with his mate Laurie Morgan, who years later would become the Olympic equestrian team captain and win the gold medal with Bill in the team event. When Bill was fourteen his parents broke up and Bill decided to travel around Australia for a bit of an adventure. He did numerous jobs, such as rabbit trapper, dingo poisoner, horse breaker and shearer.

When World War II broke out, Bill joined the army. He initially joined the 2nd/22 Infantry, but because he went absent without leave Bill was left out of the infantry, which was lucky for him, as sadly his mates were massacred by the Japanese. Bill served for five years in the army, seeing action in New Guinea and New Britain then two years in Darwin.

When the war ended, Bill married Mavis and they bought a 690-acre block of land in western Victoria. Both Bill and Mavis worked very hard on the land and turned it into a profitable farm. Bill also drove trucks, broke horses and sheared sheep. 'I was a jack of all trades, but not much a master of any of them,' he says.

Bill was making a few dollars from the farm and started entering equestrian events. In 1960 at the age of 45, Bill was selected to ride for Australia at the Rome Olympics. The three-day event took place in scorching 40 degree heat. Eighteen nations entered the event and by the second day, twelve horses had fallen at the thirty-first fence. Bill was one of the fallen—he had landed on his shoulder, got back on the horse, cleared four more obstacles and finished the course. 'It was my fault, I was going too fast. I should have eased up a bit, but I didn't, I fell from the horse and it landed on top of me.'

Bill was taken to hospital with a cracked collarbone, concussion and multiple abrasions. It was a horrible accident for Bill and devastating news for the team— without a third member the team could not compete. He was told by the doctors that he could not ride a horse for at least another month. However, he had heard the dilemma of his team and, against the doctors' orders, left the hospital and rode 12 perfect jumps —all with his arm strapped to his body. Australia won gold at the 1960 Rome Olympic Games and Bill's determination and perfect ride became one of the greatest achievements in Olympic history.

Bill also became the first Australian to win the three-day Badminton competition in England. He continued to compete in equestrian events and placed seventh in the 1964 Tokyo Olympic Games. Bill received a bronze medal and was the Australian Flag Bearer at the 1968 Mexico Olympics, then went on to come fourth and sixth in the 1972 Munich Olympic Games. At the age of sixty-one he received a Bronze medal at the 1976 Montreal Olympic Games. Amazingly his sons Barry, Clarke and Wayne also competed in some of the Olympic Games with their father. At the time, no other family in Olympic history had achieved such a feat.

Bill Roycroft was an Aussie battler who bloomed late. He lifted the profile of equestrianism, not only in Australia but around the world. In 1978 at 63, Bill retired from competitive competition and was appointed to the Federation Equestrian International three-day event committee. He competed in five Olympic Games, the first when he was 45. Can you imagine if he had competed 20 years earlier?

I met Bill on his farm, which is a few hours' drive from Melbourne. He and his wife still take care of the farm, but Bill stopped riding horses when he was in his seventies, due to a few falls and broken ribs. He is a humble man, who doesn't understand any of the fuss that surrounds him. 'All I did was ride a horse', he tells me. 'Yes I reply, but it's the story about you and your horse that keeps us all in awe of you.' 'I'll tell you something; my wife deserved a medal. She was the one that looked after the farm and the children while I was overseas riding horses.' That might be the case, but I don't think any Australian would deny Bill Roycroft that medal after his incredible 1960 Rome Olympics ride.

Jim Russell

Cartoonist

JIM RUSSELL's letterhead read: 'Newspaper Cartoonist, Films, Radio, Television, Public Relations, Art, Advertising, Travel Features, Publishing and Promotions'. Although Jim succeeded in all of the above, he will be remembered most for 'The Potts' cartoon strip.

Born James Newton Russell on 26 March 1909, from a very young age Jim was interested in cartooning, his older brother Dan and father were both talented cartoonists and Jim wanted to follow in their footsteps. When Jim was young he would buy all the cartoon magazines and would practise his drawing skills.

At 15 Jim left school and found a job as a copy boy at Sydney's *Daily Guardian*. However, he was soon fired because he spent too much time visiting the art department! Shortly after, Jim obtained a job at *Smith's Weekly* newspaper; he started there as a copy boy, but wanted to become a cartoon artist. Jim's drawing abilities were not perfect so he left the paper and acquired a job at the Sydney Stadium, where he worked as an office boy and started boxing. Jim actually had five professional fights and won all of them. In between his work duties and boxing Jim would sketch the fighters of the day. One day while Jim was sketching a boxer, the head of Fox Films noticed his sketches and realised that Jim was a diamond in the rough. The executive offered Jim an unpaid job working for Fox and in return Jim would be taught to become an artist. He accepted the offer and stayed there until 1928.

Jim then started working for the *Sydney Evening News* and became Australia's youngest political cartoonist. But the world was changing; the Great Depression had hit and the *Sydney Evening News* had to close. Jim was able to get his job back at *Smith's*, where, as well as cartooning, he wrote film and sporting reviews and in 1938 was given half a page to create his comics.

Another cartoonist at *Smith's* was Stan Cross; Stan had been drawing the cartoon strip 'You & Me'. The cartoon was very popular, but in 1939 Cross decided to leave the paper due to a disagreement with the editors. This disagreement gave Jim the opportunity to take over as head cartoonist. By early 1940 he had taken over

'You & Me' and renamed it 'Mr and Mrs Potts'. Jim created a few more characters but felt that it was still missing something.

During the 1940s Jim started to write comic books and in 1947 he and his brother Dan began their own publishing company. Unfortunately, it would close three years later due to rising production costs. In 1950 *Smith's Weekly* also closed and the cartoons were taken over by the *Melbourne Herald*. Jim moved to the *Herald* and continued creating 'The Potts' family cartoons, but he still thought it needed a new family member, so Jim introduced Uncle Dick. 'Uncle Dick was good for the strip. He gave the family another dimension, he was only suppose to stay for about a week, but ended up staying for over fifty years. Uncle Dick became everyone's favourite character and I could get away with a lot through Uncle Dick,' says Jim'.

Apart from cartooning, Jim also worked as a public relations officer for the Australian Olympic Federation, appeared on numerous radio shows and was a press officer, administrator, publicist and mentor for the Australian Olympic swimming team for the 1956 Melbourne Olympic Games.

By the 1960s Jim was appearing on numerous television shows and continued to make his deadline for 'The Potts' cartoon. In 1973 Jim was asked to draft Australia's first tourism policy. By the end of the 1970s Jim had received numerous prestigious awards, including being the first Australian to be accepted into the National Cartoonist Society in the United States. In 2000 he *Guinness Book of Records* recognised Jim Russell's cartooning achievements by announcing that he held the world record for continual drawing of a comic strip by a single artist.

On 15 August 2001 Jim Russell passed away; he was still drawing 'The Potts' cartoon until the very end.

I asked Jim to pose for this memorable photo in 2001 and he told me it was the first time that Jim Russell and Uncle Dick had ever appeared together. Jim was a wonderful man, whom I have deep respect for.

Bruce Ruxton
Returned Services League executive

BRUCE RUXTON was born in Melbourne in 1926. He joined the Australian Imperial Air Force in 1943 and served in the South West Pacific, the Netherlands, East Indies and was at the landing at Balikpapan in Borneo. Ruxton then went to Japan with the British Commonwealth Occupation Force and served there for three years. 'When we got there, there were a lot of people and a lot of confusion; they didn't even know what day it was!' Ruxton returned home from Japan and left the army in 1949. 'It was a bit strange for a while; it took a while to get used to not being in the army.' Ruxton joined the Returned Services League (RSL) in 1946 while he was still serving in the AIF. Ruxton has been on the RSL State Council for 40 years and the State Executive for over 38 years. He was Deputy National President from 1988 to 1997 and has been a member of the National Executive of the RSL since 1979.

Throughout Bruce's time in the RSL he has worked eighteen-hour days, fighting for the rights of all ex-service men and women and their families, ensuring they were looked after in terms of welfare, accommodation and other related matters. For over 30 years, Bruce received hundreds of letters each week from returned ex-service men and women, asking for his help. Bruce poured his heart and soul into crusading for each and every one of them; though sadly many Australians have not seen that side of him. Throughout his life Bruce has been a controversial figure. He is famous for speaking his mind and his remarks are sometimes thought of as old fashioned. But he is not looking after twenty-year-olds, he is protecting people who fought for our country over the last ninety years. 'In a democracy, you can't go wrong if you speak out on what the majority thinks and that's what I've been doing; you can never go wrong.'

Bruce has been acknowledged for getting people back to Anzac Day marches. In 1984 the *Sun* newspaper predicted that the Anzac Day march could stop due to dwindling numbers. In response, Bruce made the dawn service at the shrine of remembrance a significant event.

'Years ago kids didn't know anything about the diggers. It's taken a long while, but they're now teaching the kids. If you don't teach the kids anything about Anzac then they won't learn.' Bruce started going to schools around Australia and slowly but surely the crowds started to gather again each year at Anzac Day. In 1987 Bruce went to Gallipoli. 'There were about 350 young people there and we were very proud of them. Three years later in 1990, 10 000 people turned up. It's a place where every kid should go; it's very much part of Australia. The younger generation have taken it on board—it's taken fifty years, but it's there—I think we've won that war.'

In 2001 Bruce had to sell his memorabilia to finance his retirement. However, he did keep one prized possession in his office—a framed photograph of his friend and hero Keith Miller. 'When I retire I just want to sit on the beach and do nothing,' he said at the time.

After 40 years' service to the RSL, and astonishingly long working days, Bruce Ruxton deserved retirement. He had fought for thousands of ex-service men and women and in most cases won. Yes, he is controversial, but Bruce Ruxton came from a generation that stood up for what they believed in. If he has something to say, he says it—it's what he believes in.

'I've got more people on my side than against me, I've got a lot of supporters out there, but I've also taken a belting over the years. If you throw grenades, son, you've got to expect some back.'

I met Bruce Ruxton in 2002 at his office. It was old and small and Ruxton had hundreds of letters neatly filed away that he was still working on. Even during our interview he was opening up letters from people who were asking for his help—he took note of every single one of them. He was still working eighteen-hour days, even though he was due for retirement very soon. Bruce was never paid for his duties as president, only receiving a car and travelling expenses. If only there were more Bruce Ruxtons in this world.

Dame Margaret Scott
Founder, Australian Ballet School

CATHERINE MARGARET MARY SCOTT (Margaret) was born in Johannesburg, South Africa on 26 April 1922. At the age of three she already knew she wanted to become a dancer; she started lessons and showed tremendous natural skill. At just sixteen Margaret left for London to join the Sadler's Wells School and Ballet. She then worked with the Ballet Rambert in London. She was a principal from 1943 until 1948 and was chosen to tour Australia and New Zealand in 1947 with the company.

Margaret enjoyed her time in Australia and remained here permanently when the Rambert Company returned to London. She based herself in Melbourne and started dancing with the National Theatre Ballet Company, of which she became a foundation member. In 1952 Margaret returned to London and worked with choreographer John Cranko in his then experimental dance group. Margaret was then asked to be the assistant director of the Ballet Rambert School, but declined and returned to Australia in 1953 with Derek Denton, who she married that same year.

In the early 1950s there was no Australian ballet school, so Margaret founded her own and began teaching. She also held classes for professional dancers, enabling them to maintain their skills between productions. Margaret's school became popular and she realised that if ballet was to grow in Australia she needed a larger school. She contacted Dr HC 'Nugget' Coombs, then chairman of the Elizabethan Theatre Trust and Governor of the Reserve Bank. Coombs was a highly respected person with many influential friends. Margaret told Coombs that there was a need to expand ballet in Australia and that she wanted to start a national ballet school. Coombs agreed and with the help from the federal government and JC Williamson's Ltd Trust, the Australian Ballet School was established in 1963.

Margaret was the founder and director of the school from 1963 until 1990. Her job was to find talented dancers, work with them and turn them into professional dancers. However, Margaret didn't just teach dancing; she had the ability to pick other talents that her students pursued and hone their skills in other creative areas.

One example is Graeme Murphy, who has become one of Australia's leading choreographers and director of the Sydney Dance Company. In 1992 Murphy persuaded Dame Margaret out of retirement to dance the role of Clara in his version of *The Nutcracker*. Margaret was apprehensive as she had not danced professionally for 40 years, but she was brilliant, performing the role again in 1994 and then in the 2000 season at the age of 78. Dame Margaret had not lost any of her skill or grace on stage.

Dame Margaret had the rare ability to see talent before anyone else, She would nurture and advise students on how to perform to their best abilities. Many of her dancers and other creative performers have worked in numerous productions in Australia and around the world.

Dame Margaret was also ahead of her time as a director; she hired a counsellor to help the students with the mental strain of the heavy workload and encouraged the students to take up other interests such as drama and music so that they would not lose interest in dancing. Dame Margaret not only made the school into one of the most credible and famous schools in the world; she also propelled Australian ballet onto the world stage.

In 1981 Margaret Scott was made a Dame of the British Empire for services to dance and dance education. She has received many other awards over the years including Honorary Life Member of the Australian Ballet School in 1988 and the Australian Dance Award for Lifetime Achievement in 1998. She continues to take a keen interest in Australian ballet.

I took this photo of Dame Margaret in 2002. I found her to be a warm and generous person. She had such a sense of style about her—the way she moved and spoke was so graceful. I have never seen her perform. Nevertheless, just by meeting her I can only imagine her presence on stage would be mesmerising. A great lady and the perfect Dame.

Harry Seidler

Architect

HARRY SEIDLER was born in Vienna in 1923. From 1933 to 1938 Seidler attended Wasagymnasium School in Vienna. When World War II broke out in Vienna the Seidler family moved to England, where Harry studied at Cambridge Technical College. From England Harry moved to Canada, then to the United States where he studied at Harvard University under Professor Walter Gropius. After that, Harry studied at Black Mountain College in North Carolina, USA, completing a design course under Josef Albers.

In 1948 Harry travelled to Rio de Janeiro and spent some time working with Oscar Niemeyer. During his time travelling the world studying and working, Harry's parents moved to Sydney, Australia. In 1948 Seidler came to visit his parents and decided to call Australia home. In 1949 Harry started his private practice in Sydney. The first house that he designed was for his mother, The Rose Seidler House. It was to become one of Seidler's most famous designs; situated in Turramurra its modern design stands out from most of the other European houses that make up the suburb. With his upbringing in Europe and studies in the United States, Canada and England, Seidler brought to Australia new and innovative designs, but he first had to convince the local councils and residents that his modern masterpieces were what Australians wanted.

By 1961 Harry had established himself as a controversial architect. His designs were very different from to what Australians were used to—fibro houses in the suburbs as opposed to city living. Many Australians were not ready for his changes. Harry did not let people's opinion get in his way, and designed the Blues Point Tower, which stands alone on McMahons Point. At the time of its completion in the early 1960s, Sydneysiders were outraged, but like most masters, Harry was ahead of his time. The Blues Point Tower came out of the ground like a beam of light, situated on stunning Sydney Harbour. The Blues Point Tower has been a talking point for over 40 years and has also had many celebrity tenants. Most importantly it is part of Sydney's historic architecture.

Harry Seidler is one of those people who seems always to be ahead of his time. His designs still cause debate and controversy. Harry has designed many buildings around Australia, mainly in Sydney but his work is more appreciated overseas than here. This doesn't bother him: 'A good design doesn't date,' he says. And for Seidler his buildings have been testimony to that legacy—many of his buildings are now considered icons. Harry has received numerous awards from all over the world and in 1987 Seidler was awarded the companion of the Order of Australia.

In 1988 Rose Seidler House was acquired by the Historic Houses Trust of NSW and is open to the public in all of its original glory. In 2003 there was a plan by the Royal Australian Institute of Architects heritage committee to have thirteen of Seidler's buildings placed on the state's heritage list, including the infamous Blues Point Tower. It has only been in recent years that a lot of us have caught up with his modern way of thinking and living. Just look around at all of the apartments being developed now—Seidler was designing buildings just like them 40 years ago!

I met Harry Seidler and his wife Penelope in 2003 at his North Sydney home/office. I couldn't believe how inviting and kind he was. Harry showed me around his home and even showed me plans of the new projects he was working on around the world. Love or hate his designs, there is no doubt that Harry Seidler is one of the most influential architects in Australian history.

Jeffrey Smart

Artist

JEFFREY SMART is an artist who paints ordinary things and turns them into extraordinary things. For most artists, painting airports, street signs, oil drums, and playgrounds would seem very boring. But for Jeffrey these are obvious choices. He makes the boring exciting and the exciting a masterpiece. Jeffrey Smart was born in Adelaide in 1921. From a very young age he wanted to be an architect, he was fascinated by the environment and manmade structures. Nevertheless Jeffrey decided against being an architect and chose to be an artist. He studied at the South Australian School of Arts and Crafts from 1937 to 1941 under Ivor Hele. It was during this time that Jeffrey became a junior teacher at Adelaide High School.

After graduating from art school in 1941 Jeffrey became an art teacher at Goodwood Boys Technical School, where he taught for four years. But it was his own art that Jeffrey wanted to pursue, Jeffrey like many other Australian artists wanted to travel overseas to see other artist's works.

In 1946, Jeffrey placed an advertisement in the *Adelaide Advertiser* which said, 'the Jeffrey Smart School of landscape painting has two vacancies for the coming term. Intending students should apply immediately.' At the time of the advertisement the art class did not exist but soon after the ad was published Jeffrey was running two classes a week. This gave Jeffrey extra money and more freedom to create his own art. By 1948 Jeffrey Smart had made a name for himself as an Australian artist, he had exhibited in Adelaide where the Art Gallery of South Australia bought one of his paintings. The Art Gallery of NSW in Sydney and the National Gallery of Victoria in Melbourne also purchased paintings. At this time Jeffrey was also receiving an income from teaching at the art school. It was time for Jeffrey to travel overseas.

In 1949, Jeffrey arrived in Britain before moving to France, where he studied at La Grand Chaumiere and then at the Academic Montmartre. Modern artist Dorrit Black had a major influence on Smart's work. Jeffrey attended Black's studio lessons, which helped develop his work and are still an influence on him today. After his studies Smart moved to Ischia on the Bay of Naples, where he painted with fellow artists Michael Shannon, Jacqueline Hick and Donald Friend. In 1963 the Tate Gallery held an exhibition of Australian artists and Jeffrey was included in the exhibition. This led to his first overseas solo exhibition in Rome in 1965. It was due to this overseas exposure that Jeffrey became known as an international artist. He left Australia permanently in 1963 and purchased a 300-year-old Tuscan mansion near Arezzo in Italy.

Based full-time in Italy, Jeffrey found more time and freedom to create his own modern and unique work.

Jeffrey's work continues to be shown in exhibitions and major galleries around the world; he has achieved international fame as an artist, which very few Australian artists have done. Jeffrey's work has become so highly sort after that when he does have an exhibition, whether it is in Europe, the United States or Australia, his work is sold prior to opening night.

Jeffrey continues to live and work in Italy and continues to exhibit his work worldwide.

In 2001, while my girlfriend and I were travelling through Europe, I had contacted Jeffrey and organised a meeting at his house. We left Florence, spent two hours on a train ride to Arezzo, then a further 30 minutes in a taxi. Eventually we ended up at Jeffrey's house where we were greeted by two peacocks. I completed the photo shoot and the day ended with Jeffrey playing the piano for us and a few of his friends. It was to say the least a beautiful day in a magical house.

Ted Smout

World War I veteran

Edward David Smout was born on 5 January 1898 in Brisbane. Ted, as he liked to be called, had a great childhood. 'As a young boy I used to go down to the park and watch the talkies.' Ted would walk three miles (nearly 5km) to and from school every day, which kept him very fit and healthy.

In 1915, when Ted was just 17, he joined the army: 'Most of my mates had joined the army. Most of them had already gone to war; I'd left school at 14 and worked. So I was pretty mature when I was 17. If you didn't join you'd get a white feather to represent that you were a coward. I told the army that I was 18 and they didn't ask for a birth certificate so I was on my way.' Ted joined the 41st Battalion, which left for South Africa then on to England. 'We were all excited and strangely enough, we were worried that the war would be finished before we got there. We spent about seven days in South Africa and then sailed for England. To entertain ourselves, we would play two-up and bingo, both illegal to play at the time. The sergeant used to walk up and down the decks, trying to catch us playing one of the games. If we'd been caught we would've been charged, so we used to have a man looking out for him. When the searg came around the corner we would stop playing and give him a smile—he never caught us!'

Ted ended up fighting on the Western Front, serving in the Army Medical Corps. He witnessed horrific casualties that haunted him for the rest of his long life. 'When we arrived in France in 1916 it was the coldest winter in history. The food was frozen, the trenches were freezing, but somehow we got used to it. Because food was so scarce, people started stealing it—a sergeant was stealing food but he got caught and served six months in gaol.'

Smout was involved in some very brutal and bloody battles, the worst being the battle of Passchendaele. 'The ground was soft and wet and because of this some of the shells wouldn't detonate. We were knee-deep in mud and to move from place to place we would have to walk on wooden boards. If the boards got shot someone would have to replace them so we could continue walking. The conditions were very bad—the trenches were infested with rats as big as cats and most of the men were itching because of body lice. It was very bad.'

Smout had luck on his side: 'We were just behind the front line when the British Military put a heavy gun 100 yards behind us. A German plane went over and spotted it and dropped artillery around us and directly onto the heavy gun. It killed the major, but I was lucky and didn't get hurt. Some days later a 200 pound bomb dropped straight through the roof of a house that we used as a rest house. It landed on the top of a French man who was lying in bed, broke both of his legs and rolled off him, it didn't detonate.'

Although Ted witnessed some horrific moments in World War I, he also had some interesting adventures. Most of his memories are of being in France during those dreadful years: 'I saw the Red Baron shot down by a machine gunner. I was one of the first there—he had his famous cross around his neck. I took out my knife and cut a piece of mahogany from the cockpit of his plane, for a souvenir. Everybody was taking souvenirs, but nobody took his cross. He killed a lot of people, so when I saw him lying there dead, I didn't feel sorry for him.'

When Ted returned from World War I he had shell shock and suffered a physical and mental breakdown. He spent three months working as a jackaroo to try to get his physical health back, but the war left him with horrible memories. 'War achieves nothing. I felt that I didn't serve a purpose. The war to end all wars doesn't happen. All those young men died for nothing.'

Ted passed away aged 106 in 2004. He was given a state funeral.

Ted Smout wanted to be remembered for his work in the community—he was a member of numerous clubs including the Red Cross and Rotary. 'I hope that I made some sort of difference in the community,' Ted told me, when I met him at his house and took this photo in 2002. He was 104 and was living on his own, still doing his own taxes, looking after himself and his house. Ted's memory was remarkable and he was very proud to be one of the last surviving World War I veterans.

Dame Joan Sutherland

Opera singer

JOAN SUTHERLAND was born in Sydney on 7 November 1926. When she was a child she used to listen to her mother play the piano and sing. Her mother used to encourage Joan by accompanying her when she sang, Joan would imitate her mother and dreamed of one day becoming an opera star. While at school Joan tried out for the choir but did not get in, as she was told that her voice was too loud and that it would drown out the other children's voices.

After completing school Joan got a job as a secretary, but it was singing that she dreamed of. At nineteen, life for Sutherland was about to change—she won free singing lessons and finetuned her voice. After saving some money, Joan and her mother went to London to see if Joan could make it onto the world stage; her dream like many others was to sing at Covent Garden. An unknown from Australia, she tried out for the Covent Garden Company, but failed four times. However, her persistence paid off and she was able to begin working for the famed company, earning ten pounds a week.

About the same time as Joan arrived in London, another young Australian found himself in London, with the dream of working in opera. Richard Bonynge was a talented pianist, who loved opera, and had worked with Joan in Australia in 1951 on their farewell tour before he headed off to the United Kingdom. Once in London, Joan and Richard started seeing each other and in 1954 they were married, creating one of the most famous partnerships in opera history. From early on, Richard knew that his wife was gifted with greatness. He would play pieces on the piano in a higher pitch than usual; Sutherland would sing higher and train her voice without jeopardising it.

By 1952 Joan was singing small roles at Covent Garden and continued to do so for a number of years. Richard kept his wife's voice in constant training and in 1959 Joan sang the lead role of Lucia di Lammermoor. This role made her an instant celebrity; from then on Joan embarked on an international career. Soon after, a dangerous medical condition threatened to rob Joan's superb voice and she had to undergo surgery. Joan was not allowed to speak, let alone sing for three weeks. However, she recovered well and to this day no other singer has kept such an extremely challenging part in her repertoire for so many years. In fact, Joan sang Lucia in Barcelona in 1988.

In 1959 the producers at Decca Music realised that Joan was going to be an international opera star, so they signed her to a record deal and captured some of her greatest live performances. In 1960 Joan made her Italian debut at La Fenice in Handel's *Alcina*. She went on to star in almost sixty different operas and graced the stage in every major concert hall in the world. Between 1965 and 1974 Joan toured with her own opera company.

In 1975 Joan Sutherland was made a Dame for her outstanding contribution to opera. After more than 40 years as one of the world's leading opera stars, Dame Joan chose the Sydney Opera House for her last performance in 1990. Dame Joan then appeared as a guest performer in London's Covent Garden performing 'Home, Sweet Home' as an encore. As our other opera dame, Dame Nellie Melba, before her.

Dame Joan Sutherland and Richard Bonynge have retired to their home in Switzerland, but often visit Sydney, where I met Joan Sutherland on her seventy-first birthday in 1997. I was amazed at how gracious she was, letting me spend over an hour with her on her birthday; the day was full of phone calls and flowers from friends all over the world and she sat and read birthday cards, posing for my photos, while her grandson rode his skateboard in and out of the kitchen. It was, I guess, an ordinary birthday, but that's what made it so extraordinary.

Rod Taylor

Actor

LONG BEFORE Russell Crowe or Nicole Kidman there was Rod Taylor. Born Rodney Sturt Taylor in Sydney on 11 January 1930, Rod had very creative parents. His mother Mona was a writer of plays and children's books and his father picked up work as an architectural draftsman. Rod would sketch alongside him for hours. After finishing school in 1944, Rod attended East Sydney Technical and Fine Arts College. 'You know, I do a lot of painting, but most people only know me for my acting,' Rod told me in 2003.

Rod was first introduced to acting when he captained the Australian surf club. 'I met a lot of actors there and I got the acting bug. I gave up art and became an actor myself.' Rod started acting on Australian radio, then moved into amateur theatre. However, it was only after seeing Laurence Olivier in a performance of *Richard III* that Rod decided to become a professional actor. 'After seeing him, I knew I would never be anything but an actor.' Rod worked in a store during the day designing and painting backdrops to pay for his studies in acting at night. His first professional performance was in George Bernard Shaw's *Misalliance*. Soon after, he auditioned for radio programs where he worked with Australian great Queenie Ashton. She said of Rod: 'I knew immediately that we had found magic.'

By 1953 Rod was in dozens of radio programs and had won the prestigious Rola award for radio acting. The award carried some prize money and Rod planned to go to England, but instead was encouraged by his fellow actors to try his luck in America. On his arrival he was met by representatives of a powerful Hollywood agency. 'I guess they were expecting a cross between Marlon Brando and Rock Hudson. Then I stepped off the plane in my tight Australian suit and their faces fell, visibly. I thought, 'Okay, you don't like me. I'll stay!' Producer Hall Wallis looked at me. Maybe he was expecting Gregory Peck or something because he said, 'Who is this bum with the broken nose?' 'I told him to stuff it and I lived on the beach, catching fish for my food.'

Rod did a screen test for the Rocky Graziano story *Somebody Up There Likes Me* but didn't get the part. The part eventually went to Paul Newman. However, some good did come out of the audition. Rod's Bronx accent was so good that he was cast as the Bronx Boy in *The Catered Affair*. The screen test was a blessing in disguise; MGM put Rod on a contract at $450 per week. Soon after, he landed supporting roles in movies such as the 1956 classic *Giant*, starring Elizabeth Taylor, Rock Hudson and James Dean. Although his first few movies were small parts, Rod was gaining experience from his fellow actors. 'I'd much rather turn down a starring role in a bad picture and do a small role in a very good picture.'

Rod's first big break came in 1960, when he accepted the leading role in the what is now a cult classic, *The Time Machine*. That same year, Rod accepted a lead role in a television series called *Hong Kong*. In doing so, he became the highest paid actor in a one-hour show at the time. After the success of *The Time Machine* and *Hong Kong*, Rod was offered the lead in Alfred Hitchcock's classic 1963 *The Birds*. It is regarded as one of Hitchcock's finest movies and one of Taylor's better roles. 1963 proved to be a good year for Rod Taylor. Not only did he star in *The Birds*, but he was offered a major role alongside Elizabeth Taylor and Richard Burton in *The VIPs*. Rod played an Australian, and the film was a huge success.

From 1954 to 1998, Rod Taylor appeared in over 50 movies. He has also appeared in many television shows and television movies, such as *Murder She Wrote* and *Walker Texas Ranger*. Rod Taylor is a Hollywood legend.

'I figure if the men in the audience want to have a drink with you and the women want to sleep with you, then you've made it,' Rod said in a 1967 interview. Rod Taylor did make it. He may not have lived in Australia for over 50 years but he is, and always will be, one of Australia's legends.

Rod Taylor has to be one of the most genuine people I have ever met. I originally met him in his home in LA in 1999. Rod has been extraordinarily supportive of this project and has been true to his word. I took this photo in 2004, while he was in Australia on holidays.

The Seekers

Musicians

THE SEEKERS—Athol Guy, Keith Potger and Bruce Woodley—formed in 1962 as a trio, but they were still searching for another member. Athol Guy was working in an advertising agency and heard about a girl who worked at the same agency who could sing. Judith Durham tried out for the boys and they instantly knew they had found their fourth member. The Seekers started playing at a coffee bar named the Treble Clef on Monday nights. Soon The Seekers were turning Monday nights at the Treble Clef into busy nights—a bar full of customers eagerly would wait to see and hear them.

Before long The Seekers were signed to W&G records and released their first LP, *Introducing The Seekers*. The LP certainly introduced The Seekers to the Australian public; soon after the band was booked to appear on numerous television shows. One show in particular would help launch their career; Graham Kennedy's hot show *In Melbourne Tonight*. The show would be a turning point for the band, but first they had to leave for a working holiday on the *Fairstar* cruise ship, where they were to perform nightly to the passengers.

On their arrival in the United Kingdom on 21 May 1964 the band met up with booking agent Eddie Jarrett. Their intention was only to stay in London for a brief period. Jarrett had booked acts for many years and knew that there was something special about The Seekers. Eddie presented the band's performance on *In Melbourne Tonight* to the producers of the *Tonight Show*, which aired on the BBC. The producers instantly booked the band, and a few days later, due to some cancellations, they were also booked to play at the London Palladium. Jarret did not want his new act to leave; he convinced them that London was the place to launch their international singing careers. The Seekers agreed. They continued playing television shows, but were eager to record.

Jarrett called the three boys into his office one day and told them that he had found a song for them to record. With Durham in a dentist chair listening by phone, The Seekers heard 'I'll Never Find Another You', which had originally been recorded by Tom Springfield. On 4 November 1964 The Seekers recorded the song at Abbey Road Studios. By February 1965 the song had reached number one on the United Kingdom charts, number 1 on the Australian charts and number 3 in the United States, selling over 2 million copies. The next single, 'A World of Our Own', reached number 1 in the United Kingdom charts, number 2 in Australia and number 15 in the United States. The band then released the album *A World Of Our Own* and released their third single, 'The Carnival is Over'. It became another number 1 hit for the band, at its pinnacle selling over 90,000 copies a day! In 1966 they toured the United Kingdom, New Zealand and Australia and released their next album *Come the Day*. The Seekers also re-recorded 'Morningtown Ride', which reached number 1. In 1967 Capitol Records in the United States released *Come the Day* under the title *Georgie Girl* and released the title track as a single. In February 1967 *Georgie Girl* reached number 1 on the American charts.

The Seekers were the first Australian band in history to have a number 1 hit on the United States charts. By 1968 they were one of the biggest bands in the world, after sell-out tours, number one hits, an Academy Award nomination and being named Australians of the Year; The Seekers had the world at their feet. However, all was not what it seemed and Judith Durham announced to the band that she was leaving at the end of their tour. On 9 July 1968 the BBC aired a special titled *Farewell The Seekers* and with that they were gone. EMI released *The Best of The Seekers*, which reached number 1 in the United Kingdom and stayed in the British top 40 charts for three years.

For the next twenty-five years the members of The Seekers worked on solo projects: Bruce Woodley wrote the classic song 'I am Australia'. In 1993 The Seekers, due to huge demand, made a sucessful comeback.

I met The Seekers in their hotel in 2003 on the morning after one of their shows; I approached each member and made my proposal, one by one. After a nervous few hours of waiting I approached them as they were leaving their hotel—I rounded them up and did a very quick photo shoot.

Colin Thiele

Author

COLIN THIELE was born on 4 August 1920 in Eudunda, South Australia. Colin lived on a farm near Eudunda and went to the local school, which at the time had only fifteen students. 'On wet days only a handful of kids would turn up for school, and the teacher would read stories to us, sometimes all day. Our library only had about twenty books. I loved reading so I read all of the books, then when I was 11, I decided to write my own book. It was called *Blackbeard the Pirate*. I later burnt it because I wasn't happy with it.'

Colin was interested in languages at an early age; his parents spoke German and Colin became fascinated with words. In the 1930s the Great Depression hit and Colin knew that he was not going to get any work on the land, so he enrolled at the University of Adelaide, where he studied to become a teacher. When Colin had finished his studies, he served in WW II in the air force. After the war Colin returned to Adelaide, got married and began teaching. Following ten years of teaching Colin was offered a job at Wattle Park Teachers College; he accepted and in 1965 became principal of the college. In 1973 Colin was promoted to director of the college and held that position until 1980, when severe arthritis forced him to retire.

Throughout Colin's teaching career he continued to write. He started writing poetry and wrote his first poetry book in 1945, during the war. From there Colin started writing short stories for *The Bulletin*. As time progressed Colin wrote books while still teaching. While travelling on a ship to San Francisco, Colin wrote the book *Sun on the Stubble*: 'I wasn't interested in playing games on the ship, so I spent the entire time writing.' Writing was Colin's hobby and was not his means of living. Thiele would lecture, teach and run the school in the day and write at night between 10 pm and 1 am.

In 1961 the Thieles took a holiday to Coorong with family friend John Bailey. Bailey was an artist who wanted to paint the Murray Mouth and surrounding areas. 'Bailey said to me, "I've got a vision of a lonely boy in that vast environment, possibly with a storm coming up, he's a sort of storm boy."' Colin thought that he could write a book about Bailey's vision. After their holiday Colin had just three weeks before school went back in the new year. In just three weeks Colin wrote *Storm Boy*. 'I gave it to the publishers and they seemed to like it, so they published it.' Producer Matt Carroll convinced Colin that he could make a good movie out of his book and in 1977 the South Australian Film Commission made the film *Storm Boy*. The movie was shown all around the world. Colin started receiving pelican ornaments and thousands of letters from people all around the world, many who actually thought that Colin himself was storm boy. The book *Storm Boy* is now in its fortieth edition and has sold millions of copies all around the world.

When Colin retired from teaching in 1980, he became a full-time writer. From areas as diverse as children's, poetry, history, fiction, education, environment and biographies; Colin has written them all. Colin wrote the first biography on famed artist Sir Hans Heysen. Thiele took a year's unpaid leave from teaching and spent a lot of time with Heysen trying to write the biography.

Colin, now in his mid-eighties, continues to write and has won numerous literary awards in Australia and around the world. His work has been translated and is available around the globe. Incredibly Colin has had over 100 books published—not bad for an author who didn't start writing full-time until 1980.

When I met Colin in 2004 I actually needed directions from five different people to find his home in Queensland. I found him to be a very kind and warm man, with a great sense of humour and once we had completed the photos and interview Colin insisted (even with his arthritis) on drawing me a map to get back. It was so detailed that I asked him to sign it for me, as it looked more like a piece of art than a map. It was very clever and precise, just like Colin and his books.

Peter Thompson
Golfer

PETER THOMPSON was born on 23 August 1929 in Brunswick, Victoria. The Thompson family home was situated near the Royal Park Golf Course. As a young boy Thompson used to caddy there and work on his golfing technique. At just 13 Thompson won his first golfing competition at the Royal Park Golf Course.

At the age of eighteen Peter won the Victorian Amateur Championship. He was a natural golfer, but needed guidance to perfect his technique; he found that guidance in Harry Young, who was a golf enthusiast. Young first saw Peter playing when he was just 15 and knew that he was witnessing a champion in the making. Young wanted Peter to become a professional golfer but Peter wasn't sure if golf was going to be his chosen profession. Peter had won a scholarship to Brunswick Technical School and completed a four-year course in applied science to become a chemist. After completing his studies Peter began working as a rubber technologist for Spalding. As luck would have it Peter's job required him to test golf balls and clubs.

In April 1949, after a conversation with golfing legend Norman von Nida, Peter went to Sydney to play in the McWilliams Wine Golf Tournament. Peter finished third behind von Nida and Ossie Pickworth. Von Nida encouraged Peter to give up his day job and become a professional golfer; eventually it was the lure of money that helped Peter decide. 'In my case the carrot was the promise of money, and at nineteen, nothing looked sweeter.'

Peter turned professional on 24 April 1949. By 1950 Peter had won the New Zealand Open and come second to von Nida at the Australian Open, Peter's final round of 66 broke the Kooyong Course record. In 1951 Peter defeated his mentor, von Nida, to win the Australian Open. The golfing world knew that they had a champion in the making and within a short period of time, Peter had mastered all of the game's techniques; however, he had also kept his natural ability and with this combination Peter was almost unstoppable.

In 1954 Peter played in the British Open. He'd played in the Open three times before; in 1951 he had finished sixth, second in 1952 and 1953. Peter was convinced that he was going to win the prestigious title. On the sixteenth hole, Peter was trapped deep in a bunker; he hit the ball to land only half a metre from the hole. Peter later would be quoted as saying: 'That was the finest stroke I'd ever played in my life.' Peter went on to win the British Open, becoming the first Australian to win the title.

Thompson went on to win five British Opens (1954, 1955, 1956, 1958 and 1965). Peter notes his win in the 1965 British Open as his greatest win of the five because: 'I had the world's best against me.' The best being Arnold Palmer, Jack Nicklaus and defending champion Tony Lema. Peter's three consecutive wins at the British Open was the first hat-trick since the 1800s, and still has not been achieved by any other golfer. Peter won three Australian Opens (1951, 1967 and 1972), two Dunlop Masters (1962 and 1968), nine New Zealand Opens (1950, 1951, 1953, 1955, 1959, 1961, 1965, 1966 and 1971) plus numerous tournaments in between.

When Peter Thompson retired after the Australian Open in 1979, he was considered one of the greatest golfers in the history of the game. After his retirement Peter continued to dominate the world of golf by winning numerous seniors events. Peter then went into the business side of golf by starting a company that designs golf courses for Australia and other countries.

I met Peter Thompson in Melbourne in 2000 at his office. He kindly suggested that we go downstairs where there was better light and more room. When we finished the photoshoot, Thompson went back upstairs to design another golf course.

Charles 'Bud' Tingwell

Actor

CHARLES 'BUD' Tingwell and I have something in common. No, I'm not an actor, producer or director. We were both born and raised in the beachside suburb of Coogee and are both photographers. But that's where our similarities end.

Born Charles William Tingwell in 1923 and nicknamed Bud by his family, Bud went to Coogee Public School, then Sydney Grammar. Bud received his first acting part in 1940, when he was still at school. He played the character of Bob Cherry on a Sydney radio serial *Magnet Stories*. From there Bud became a junior radio announcer for 2CH.

But before Bud could establish himself as an actor World War II came calling. Bud joined the RAAF, flying Mosquitoes and Spitfires in over 75 missions. Bud's main task was to photograph the enemy wherever they were, even if entrenched in the enemy's terrain, which was exceptionally dangerous. Luckily for his squadron they didn't encounter too many casualties. Ironically Bud's first speaking part was in the film *Smithie* and Bud got the part of a control officer; as long as he agreed to wear his own air force uniform. From there his career took off and in 1947 he was chosen to play the lead role in the movie *Always Another Dawn*.

Bud was definitely on his way to becoming a star. He worked in movies, stage and radio. In 1952, 20th Century Fox signed Bud to play a role in the Hollywood movie *The Desert Rats* co starring with Chips Rafferty, James Mason and Richard Burton. The studio directors were so impressed with Tingwell's ability as an actor that they offered him a seven-year movie contract. Although most actors would have jumped at the opportunity, Tingwell didn't want to be stuck doing movies in the United States for seven years. He turned down the contract and returned to Australia to further his career back home. He continued to work in radio, movies and theatre; but it was not long before he was to leave Australian shores again for continuing work.

In 1958 Bud and his wife Audrey left for England to finish some scenes for *The Shiralee*, which starred fellow Australian and Academy Award winner Peter Finch. It would be a working holiday that would change Bud and Audrey's lives. Bud was so in demand as an actor in the United Kingdom that he and his wife ended up staying in London for 16 years. Bud had never been busier. He was the lead character in all four of Agatha Christie's Miss Marple films starring Dame Margaret Rutherford, and he also played the lead in the BBC radio drama series *Overload Patrol*. In between radio and the movies, Bud played the lead in *There's a Girl in My Soup* for two years at London's West End. Not wanting to limit his already established career, Bud also lent his voice for characters in the 1960s cult TV classic *The Thunderbirds*.

Bud returned to Australia in 1972 and continued to work in television, radio, theatre and the movies. From starring in the production to writing, producing or directing, Bud Tingwell's career has not slowed down. It almost seems as if Bud Tingwell has been in every television show that has ever been made. He has starred and featured in such notable television shows and movies as *Homicide*, *Prisoner*, *Breaker Morant*, *Puberty Blues*, *Neighbours*, *Malcolm*, *Evil Angels* and *The Harp in the South*, to name but a few. Not to forget the role that made him famous with my generation, the 1997 comedy sensation *The Castle*.

You might say that *The Castle* introduced Tingwell to a new, younger audience; Bud was once again on a roll. He backed up *The Castle* with another recent comedy, *The Wog Boy*. With more than sixty years of experience in the entertainment industry, Tingwell can be thought of as an Australian cross between Milton Berle and Bob Hope. Now in his eighties, Bud has far from slowed down; he continues to be in demand by the Australian public and has recently released his autobiography *Bud*.

I met Bud in 2000 after one of his shows called *The Carer*. Before the photo shoot I noticed an area full of beautiful stones next to the theatre, so I asked Bud if we could possibly go next door for some shots. He happily agreed to go down to that area and I photographed him from above.

Nancy Wake

World War II heroine

NANCY WAKE was born in Roseneath in Wellington, New Zealand on 13 August 1912. Nancy and her family moved to Sydney when she was just twenty months old. She was the youngest of six children and because of the age gap between her and her other siblings, she became fiercely independent—a loner and a rebel with a good imagination. Nancy left Australia when she was in her early twenties. She travelled around Europe; then, being fluent in French, eventually ended up in Paris, finding work as a journalist. Nancy enjoyed the independence and carefree lifestyle of the French, but like most people living in Europe in the late 1930s her life was about to radically change for the worse.

World War II broke out in 1939 and by 1940 Germany had invaded France. Nancy worked for the French resistance, who helped thousands of people escape from capture by the Germans. Nancy's first task was to smuggle messages and food to underground groups in southern France. It was an extremely dangerous job, and spelt disaster for her if the Gestapo caught her. In fact it was the Gestapo who codenamed Nancy 'The White Mouse' because they could never catch her.

In November 1939 Nancy married Frenchman Henri Fiucca. He later urged her to leave France, otherwise she would be killed: 'He was the love of my life and it was the most difficult thing I have done in my entire life,' she says.

By 1943 Nancy was the number one target on the Gestapo's most wanted list. There was a five million franc price tag on her head; knowing this Nancy escaped to London where she trained as a spy. Within a year of leaving France, the Gestapo had killed and tortured Henri in an attempt to find her. Nancy returned to France stronger and more determined to fight against Hitler's regime. Her training included weapons handling, unarmed combat and parachuting.

At the age of 29 Nancy had command of over 7000 Resistance fighters, whose jobs were to do hit-and-run harassment attacks on the Germans, and weaken their army. This type of attack was very effective as when it was time for the Allies to attack with the full strength of their troops, the Germans would be more easily defeated. 'I found when it came to killing I was as good as the next man,' says Nancy. In one instance Nancy had to silence a guard; she was just going to give him a hit on the head to knock him out but as she approached him he saw her and opened his mouth to scream. Without even thinking, she clamped her arm under his jaw and snapped his neck. The guard slumped against her, dead. Nancy knew that it was either her or the enemy.

Of all of Nancy's great triumphs she is most proud of the gruelling 200-kilometre bike ride she miraculously did to reach another radio operator, after her group lost their radio when German troops raided them. This mission was imperative, as messages to organise the distribution of weapons and other supplies had to be sent via radio phones. This example gives an insight into why Nancy Wake is the most decorated servicewoman of World War II.

After the war Nancy worked in Paris for the British Foreign Office Passport Control for a couple of years, then returned to Australia for a while. She then decided to move back to England where she married RAF pilot John Forward, and in 1960 they retired to Australia.

In 1997, I drove up to Port Macquarie to meet and photograph Nancy Wake. When I arrived at her humble flat I pressed her doorbell Nancy came out on her balcony and threw down the keys so I could let myself in. I found her very entertaining, particularly when telling me stories about her life—not just about World War II but also about recent occurrences. One story in particular stands out. 'A couple of weeks ago, at about 2:50 am I heard a noise in the apartment building, I went out to see what was going on, there were about three kids around 15 years of age, I asked them what they were doing. They got scared and ran away, I followed them down the stairs, they panicked and couldn't open the front door so they ran out the back of the units. I followed them down and went out the front way to try to catch them as they came around. I just wanted to know where their parents were!' Nancy didn't catch them. Mind you, she was 85 years old and it was 2:50 am.

Nancy Bird Walton
Aviator

NANCY BIRD Walton may be the only person still alive today who can say that she flew with Sir Charles Kingsford Smith. Nancy Bird was born in Kew, New South Wales in 1915. As a child Nancy thought school was a waste of time and left at just 13. 'I just wanted to get on with life.' The Depression had hit, so work was very hard to find, but Nancy found work with her father and uncle who ran a general store. Nancy's father was a hard worker and expected nothing less from his children. 'I used to get up at 6am, make breakfast, then I had to carry water from the tanks outside. I would clean and scrub the house by hand, fill the kerosene lamps, help in the shop and after we closed the shop for business I'd have to do the accounting, all for just 1 pound a week!'

Nancy was very determined to learn to fly and missed out on most comforts to fulfil her dream. She learnt the ins and outs of truck engines to compliment the information in her flying books and manuals, so that she could fully understand how an engine worked. She took the first steps towards becoming a pilot when she bought herself flying goggles, a flying helmet and a leather jacket. Nancy was ready to hit the skies; all she needed now was a plane. When Nancy was fifteen a pilot by the name of Reg Annabel visited her area. He offered people a flight in his plane for 1 pound. Nancy offered him 30 shillings for the flight, a couple of loops, a spin and some turns. This flight made her more determined to fly.

Two years later Sir Charles Kingsford Smith visited her in Wingham and when Nancy was offered to fly again, she took the opportunity. When Kingsford Smith and Nancy landed, she told Kingsford Smith that she wanted to fly. He told her that he was going to open a flying school in Mascot (Sydney) and that she could attend the school.

On 11 August 1933, Nancy had her first flying lesson, with none other than Sir Charles Kingsford Smith. Nancy continued to receive flying lessons, usually from Pat Hall, who was part of Kingsford Smith's flying team. After her flying instructions Nancy was ready to fly solo.

In the 1930s planes were a novelty in Australia and very few people thought that you could make a career from flying. However, Nancy saw the future in flying. Flying was very new; it was hard for a man to be successful with this new invention, let alone a young girl!

Nancy bought a damaged Moth aeroplane and with the help of her friend and co-pilot Peggy McKillop, rebuilt the plane. Soon they were off on their maiden tour of NSW. Determined to make some money from their new-found career, they gladly accepted a women's magazine offer to have the magazine's name on the plane for ten pounds a week for three weeks. The women then flew around western NSW charging ten shillings for joy rides. Everywhere they went, people flocked to see them; not only was the plane a novelty but so were they.

All was not well, though. The trips were long and hard, they flew through treacherous conditions and had no landing strips to safely land on. At just twenty-two, Nancy decided that she had to stop her barnstorming trips across rural NSW. With the help of the president of the aero club at Narromine, Nancy purchased a new plane. She became the first Australian woman to operate an aircraft commercially, and the youngest woman in the British Empire to hold a commercial licence.

Nancy borrowed 1200 pounds from the bank and started as a freelance commercial pilot. She flew to towns that other aircraft would not stop at. Nancy soon found work with the Far West Children's Health Scheme. She would also fly nurses to people in need of medical treatment. In 1953 Nancy founded, and became the first president of, the Australian Womens Pilot Association.

In 1958 after a twenty year absence from flying Nancy flew in the Powder Puff Derby in America. At the time she was the first non-American contender; she came fifth out of 68 competitors.

I have to give a lot of credit to Nancy, as she was one of the first people to invite me to her home for this book. I rang her in early 1997 and asked: 'Are you Nancy Bird, who used to fly aeroplanes?' 'Yes, but that was a long time ago,' she replied. Since then I have spent many hours with Nancy at her home.

Dr David Warren

Inventor of the black box

W HAT'S THE first thing that investigators look for when an aeroplane crashes? They should look for Dr David Warren and thank him for his courage and sheer determination.

David Warren was born on 20 March 1925 in the Northern Territory. 'My parents wanted me to have a good education, so I was sent south, to do my schooling.' I went to university to study science.' When World War II ended David was offered a job at Sydney University, lecturing.

In 1948 David went to London and trained in rocket research. His training complete he was told: 'We've trained too many, so can we offer you a job working with jet air craft fuels?' Warren accepted and in 1952 became a principal research scientist with Aeronautical Research Laboratories in Melbourne. In 1953 the world's first jet-powered aircraft crash occurred; David thought it could have been a fuel tank explosion but could not prove it.

David had seen a miniature voice recorder and thought, 'why can't we have one of these in an aeroplane? Then we could hear what was being said in the cockpit and get data on the instruments.' David brought the idea up with some colleagues at his work. In condescending tones he was advised that if the idea was so good they themselves would have already invented it, or the Americans would have! David then drew the blueprint for the first flight data recorder, but was told by his superiors to get on with his chemistry.

Twelve months later nothing had happened. But his luck was about to change. He now had a new overseer who encouraged his idea. David wrote a report in 1954 and sent it all over the world, but surprisingly received no response. Frustrated, David purchased a recorder and went on secret flights to record the pilot and information. In 1957 his superior asked him to make a model. He was told that it was still not official, as no one in the laboratory had agreed with the idea. David asked a friend to make a model and gave him the blueprint. The plans were to filter out background noise and record data, including air speed, cabin pressure and the pilots' voices. David showed the model to the Department of Civil Aviation (DCA), who told him that there was no market for it. One day his superior was with the secretary of the UK Air Registration Board, who asked David to tell him what he was doing.

'So I said, this little tape recorder stores the last four hours of voice and instruments on the aircraft. If you have a crash you'll find this, and you'll have the answers you are looking for.' David soon found himself on a plane to England. He gave his lecture, which was received with great enthusiasm.

Back in Australia he was given five orders from Bristol Aircraft. David then took his idea to Canada, where they also thought the flight recorder was a great idea. However, his invention was still not greeted with any enthusiasm at home. The DCA said 'it had no significance to civil aviation' and the Royal Australian Air force (RAAF) said 'your device would produce more expletives than explanations. To the RAAF, the loss of aircraft is an acceptable risk.'

In 1960 after a plane crash, the board of inquiry was told about David's invention. The judge asked the DCA, 'If you had a flight data recorder on board would it have helped in your investigations?' The DCA replied yes and added that they had been working on one for five years.

'I was furious at this blatant lie, as the DCA had been our biggest barrier,' says David. The judge came back the next day and said, 'I will make it law that all our planes will be fitted with one of these by next year.' In 1961 Australia became the first country in the world to make flight recorders compulsory.

Dr Warren was further insulted by the DCA inviting a United States company to produce and market his invention. As a public servant there was nothing he could do about it. Despite eight years of work, David has never been given credit for his groundbreaking idea.

It took me years to track down Dr Warren. In the mid-1990s I rang everyone I could find who had anything to do with aviation, but no-one had heard of him! Finally by sheer luck I came across a report on Australian inventions, which listed David's last workplace. From there I was finally able to meet him in 2000.

Max Whitehead

Model/athlete

FOOTBALLER, FACTORY worker, police officer, air force pilot, chicken sexer, lifesaver, wrestler, cruise worker, milkman and, last but not least, original Chesty Bond model. That's Max Whitehead.

Max Whitehead has had a very intriguing life. Born on 2 August 1922, Whitehead completed his schooling at Manly Intermediate. While he was at school he showed an interest in rugby league—at 15 he played in the President's Cup. After school he was working in the Bushell's Coffee Factory: 'I had to stir big bowls of sugar—I got out of there pretty quick.'

Max took up playing football again. He joined North Sydney in the early 1940s and played in the Grand Final with the team in 1943. But in the 1940s it wasn't possible to make a living from football. In 1941 he joined the police force and stayed there for five years; during this time he spent about five months in the air force. After the air force Max left the police force and didn't know what to do. A friend told him that if he had been in the service he could train to do something, as a profession. 'I chose something very different—I learnt to be a chicken sexer.'

In 1947 Manly had formed a rugby league team and Max was selected in the first team. 'The day of the first game the coach said to me, "Max, you're the captain", and from that day on I was Manly's first rugby league captain.' Max played with Manly for a few years, but was not making a good living. During winter he worked as a chicken sexer, and in the summer he was a lifeguard. He won the Australian Championships for lifesaving in 1946.

However, Max was still not content—he wanted to see the world. 'I went to Jim Paul's gym; when I got there I weighed 14 stone 4 pounds, when I left I was 16 stone and ready to wrestle.' Max was offered a job as a professional wrestler in New Zealand. On one night 10 000 New Zealanders watched Whitehead wrestle. He was a very successful and popular wrestler, only losing one match. Max left for Europe, where he also became a famous wrestler in Munich. He wrestled under the character name of Dr Thomas Stanley. 'People asked me what sort of doctor I was, I told them I was a doctor of natural hydraulics and they didn't know what I was talking about—come to think of it, neither did I!'

Max left Europe and wrestled all around the United States for approximately three years. When he returned to Australia he continued to wrestle and carry out his lifesaving duties. In the mid-1950s clothing manufacturer Bonds were looking for a model who looked like their Chesty Bond cartoon character. 'I was a fit-looking bloke, with a decent sized jaw. Bonds must've thought that I looked like the cartoon character, so they hired me as their model.' Max was paid to make appearances to promote Chesty Bond singlets. He did this job for a few years and had fun being a model. 'I remember one day when the make-up artist from Bonds put a fake jaw on me. Now I had a pretty big jaw anyway, so we were driving down the street and these two ladies pulled up by the side of our car and their jaws just dropped, I must have looked ridiculous.' After modelling and working with chickens, Whitehead started working on world cruise ships; he then bought a milk run.

Max has had a full and technicoloured life. He was Manly's first rugby league captain, the Chesty Bond model, and a world famous wrestler. Now in his eighties he still exercises every day and visits his beloved Manly Surf Life Saving Club three times a week, to train in the gym, swim and run on the beach. 'I wake up, I count my blessings and I know that I'm fortunate, I've had a good life—not bad for a guy who's broke.' Max is a happy man, full of energy and life and, yes, he is broke. He doesn't even have a phone.

It took me about two years to track Max down. Finally I was able to call his next-door neighbour. I have met Max a few times over the years, the last being in 2002 at his beloved Manly Surf Life Saving Club, when I took this photo. He is exceptionally fit, fun, an avid reader, and modest. Like many Max couldn't understand 'what all the fuss was about'. When our photo shoot had ended, Max did a weightlifting workout then went for a swim. After his workout he still had the energy for a few good yarns.

Gough Whitlam

Former prime minister

GOUGH WHITLAM is possibly more famous for being dismissed as prime minister by the Governor-General than for being a politician. Born Edward Gough Whitlam on 11 July 1916 in Kew, Victoria, his father, Fred Whitlam, was a federal public servant who served as Solicitor-General. Fred had a huge influence on the young Gough, who went on to study law at the University of Sydney. During his studies World War II began so Gough joined the Royal Air Force, reaching the rank of flight lieutenant while serving as a navigator. Because of his father's influence, Gough was interested in politics from an early age. He joined the Australian Labor Party in 1945 and by 1952 Gough had been elected into the House of Representatives. But the 1950s was a dark period in the Labor years. Robert Menzies was elected prime minister in 1949 and remained so for many years. During the 1950s and 1960s the Liberal–Country Party had control of Australian politics, led by Menzies, Harold Holt, John Gorton and William McMahon.

After the 1967 election when Harold Holt defeated Arthur Calwell in a massive win, Calwell stood down as leader of the Opposition, leaving the way open for Gough to become leader. As leader, Gough took control of his party and worked on developing new policies. The then prime minister, William McMahon, was somewhat out of touch with the Australian public and the Liberal Party, which had had an iron grip over Australian politics for twenty-three years was on the decline.

Gough, on the other hand, was in his prime; he had new and exciting policies, but struggled with the conservatism of his party, and in 1966 had almost been expelled. He had proposed to abolish the White Australia Policy and wanted Australian troops out of Vietnam.

The public were listening, and felt that it was now time for a change. On 2 December 1972 Gough won the election. He wasted no time putting his policies into place. He abolished the White Australia Policy, took responsibility for tertiary education away from the states and abolished tertiary fees. Gough introduced a support benefit for single parent families, abolished the death penalty for federal crimes, reduced the voting age from 21 to 18, improved media services for immigrants (leading to the establishment of SBS), gave women equal opportunity in federal government employment, and set up the National Aboriginal Consultative Committee. Gough initiated direct federal grants to local government, a free national health system known as Medibank (now Medicare), and restored diplomatic relations with the People's Republic of China (to name but a few). Gough was a strong and confident leader and with so many changes in such a short period, the conservatives began to worry.

In May 1974 Gough won another election, but it was his spending sprees that had people wary. His government was then caught up in a scandal. The Opposition accused him of borrowing large amounts of money from Middle East governments, bypassing the Treasury and correct procedures (the Loans Affair). Gough was not popular with many politicians, especially Queensland Premier Joh Bjelke-Petersen. In 1975 Queensland Labor Senator Bert Milliner died; Bjelke-Petersen should have replaced Milliner with Labor's chosen replacement Mal Colston, but instead nominated Albert Field (a minor Labor Party member), who was willing to help Bjelke-Petersen in Gough's political demise.

The Opposition delayed consideration of the budget while Gough tried to borrow money from the banks to keep the economy and government moving. The two parties were deadlocked and Opposition leader Malcolm Fraser urged Governor-General Sir John Kerr to act. Kerr contacted Queen Elizabeth II and asked for permission to dismiss Gough. Kerr had been a Whitlam appointment, but felt he and his wife had been ignored and snubbed by him. On 11 November 1975 Gough was dismissed as prime minister of Australia.

I have met and photographed Gough Whitlam numerous times at different events. This photo was taken on Federation Day in 2001 at Centennial Park in Sydney.

RM Williams

WHEN PRIME Minister John Howard went to America in 2004 he met up with former Hollywood film star and now Governor of California Arnold Schwarzenegger. Howard greeted Schwarzenegger with a friendly smile, a handshake and a pair of RM William boots. This is how most Australians feel about RM—he is an indelible part of Australia's history.

Reginald Murray Williams was born in rural South Australia in May 1908. He left home in his teens and went bush. RM lived and learnt his bush skills from the Aborigines, and his horse and cattle skills from the people who lived on the isolated cattle stations north of the Nullarbor.

In the outback he was a lime burner, gold digger, camel boy, drover, miner and well digger to name a few, but it was his skills as a bootmaker that would make his name synonymous throughout the world.

After three years living off the land and trekking through thousands of kilometres of desert, RM had to head back to Adelaide, where his family had moved to. He did not want to leave the land and he found it very difficult to get work due to the Great Depression. Once back in Adelaide RM married Thelma Mitchell. He was not comfortable living in the city, he moved to the Flinders Rangers with his new wife and started a family.

It was during this time that a horseman by the name of Dollar Mick stopped to visit RM and his wife. Dollar Mick (real name George Smith) was a very talented craftsman and taught RM the skills he needed to be a leather craftsman. Because of his life on the land RM knew exactly what sort of high quality, practical and functional leather goods were needed for the people on the land. He started making leather goods for people on neighbouring stations.

It wasn't until RM's second child was born and contracted an eye disease that RM realised he had to turn his hobby of making leather items, such as pack saddles and boots, into a money making venture. First and foremost the RM Williams brand came out of basic needs, not fashion.

Knowing his son needed medical treatment, RM met with businessman and property mogul Sir Sidney Kidman and persuaded him to buy his pack saddles. Soon people from all over the country were sending orders to RM and he had to move back to Adelaide, where in an old iron woodshed at the back of his father's house at 5 Percy St, Prospect, RM started his business. In 2000 RM Williams opened the distinctive outback Heritage Museum on this original site.

RM's business was rapidly growing and with the help of some mates he bought an old gold mine. Luckily for him the gold mine paid off—he made millions of dollars and was able to expand his business. But there was one problem: RM wasn't happy with the life of luxury that he was leading in Adelaide. He was leading a life that was not true to him and eventually his marriage broke up. RM moved to Queensland to start over again.

'I went back to where I belonged,' he said. He remarried and had three more children (now a total of nine. His business continued to grow and today the RM Williams range of leather goods and clothes is sold around Australia and around the world. The RM Williams boots have become more famous than the man himself, and that's just the way RM liked it. He was happy on the land riding horses, which he did into his nineties. RM wrote books about his extraordinary life and also published his poetry, but it was his involvement in creating The Stockmen's Hall of Fame in Longreach, Queensland in 1988 that he became most proud of; he thought of it as a tribute to all people who lived on the land.

The iconic figure we came to know as RM passed away in his modest home in Queensland on 4 November 2003; he was 95.

When I travelled to RM's property in north Queensland in late 2002 I ended up at his son John's house first; there I was taught to crack a whip. Being a Sydney boy, I had no idea what I was doing, but John wanted to teach me something about the land. I think he was giving me an insight into his father's way of living.

Bibliography

Publications:

Lock-Weir, Tracey, 2001, *John Dowie: A Life in the Round*, Wakefield Press.

Ross, Peter, 1999, *Let's Face It: The History of the Archibald Prize*, Art Gallery of New South Wales.

Sheppard, Trish, 1984, *Australian Adventurers*, Angus & Robertson Publishers, pp:129-140, 177-186.

The New York Times July 18 2000 (on Marcus Oliphant).

Veitch, Alan and Atterton, Margot, 1984, *The Illustrated Encyclopaedia of Australian Showbiz*, Sunshine Books. Child & Henry Publishing.

Quartermaine, Peter, 1983, *Jeffrey Smart*, Gryphon Books.

Capon, Edmund, 1999, *Jeffrey Smart Retrospective at the Art Gallery of New South Wales*, Beagle Press.

Wide World of Sports, Australian Sporting Hall of Fame, 1984, Angus & Robertson Publishers, pp:219,267,272,130,189,33,170,195,236,76.

Websites:

www.bobjane.com.au

www.edwardkenna.homestead.com

www.gulpilil.com

www.johnlaws.com.au

www.geocities.com/SunsetStrip/Alley/4567/

www.rmwilliams.com.au

www.2ue.com

www.nma.gov.au/primeministers/10.htm

www.richardsimpkin.com.au